Mor

Everything You Need to Know

Copyright © 2023 by Noah Gil-Smith.

All rights reserved. No part of this book may be reproduced, distributed, or transmitted in any form or by any means, including photocopying, recording, or other electronic or mechanical methods, without the prior written permission of the publisher, except in the case of brief quotations embodied in critical reviews and certain other noncommercial uses permitted by copyright law. This book was created with the assistance of Artificial Intelligence. The content presented in this book is for entertainment purposes only. It should not be considered as a substitute for professional advice or comprehensive research. Readers are encouraged to independently verify any information and consult relevant experts for specific matters. The author and publisher disclaim any liability or responsibility for any loss, injury, or inconvenience caused or alleged to be caused directly or indirectly by the information presented in this book.

Introduction to Morocco: A Land of Rich Heritage 6

Geographical Diversity of Morocco 8

Early History and Ancient Civilizations 10

The Berbers: Indigenous People of Morocco 12

Arab Influence and the Arrival of Islam 14

Dynasties of Morocco: From Idrisids to Alawites 16

The French and Spanish Colonial Period 19

Modern Morocco: Independence and Governance 22

Moroccan Wildlife and Ecological Wonders 25

A Culinary Journey Through Moroccan Cuisine 28

The Exquisite World of Moroccan Tea 30

Tangier - Gateway to Africa and Europe 32

Casablanca - Morocco's Economic Hub 34

Marrakech - The Red City of History and Magic 37

Fes - The Spiritual and Cultural Heart 40

Rabat - The Capital of Morocco 42

Meknes - A Hidden Gem of Imperial Cities 45

Chefchaouen - The Blue Pearl of Morocco 47

Essaouira - A Coastal Gem of Tranquility 50

Sahara Desert - Mysteries of the Dunes 53

Atlas Mountains - A Trekker's Paradise 56

Moroccan Architecture: A Blend of Traditions 59

The Souks of Morocco: A Shopper's Delight 62

Moroccan Arts and Crafts 65

Music and Dance: The Rhythms of Morocco 68

Festivals and Celebrations Across the Year 71

Moroccan Hospitality: Riads and Guesthouses 74

Moroccan Dress and Traditional Attire 77

Moroccan Henna Art and Tattoos 80

Moroccan Weddings and Ceremonies 83

The Moroccan Language: Arabic and Amazigh 86

Dialects and the Role of French 89

Learning Moroccan Arabic for Travelers 92

Moroccan Literature and Poetic Traditions 95

Religion in Morocco: Islam's Influence 98

Moroccan Education and Institutions 101

Healthcare and Wellness in Morocco 103

Transportation in Morocco: Trains, Taxis, and More 106

Moroccan Etiquette and Customs 109

Safety Tips for Travelers in Morocco 112

Sustainable Tourism in Morocco 115

Excursions and Day Trips: Beyond the Cities 118

Adventure Tourism: Trekking and Desert Safaris 121

Morocco's Future: Challenges and Opportunities 124

Epilogue 127

Introduction to Morocco: A Land of Rich Heritage

Nestled in the northwest corner of Africa, Morocco is a nation that captivates the senses and intrigues the soul. It is a land where history whispers through the labyrinthine streets of ancient medinas, where the aroma of exotic spices fills the air, and where diverse landscapes paint a vivid canvas of natural beauty.

Morocco's rich heritage is a tapestry woven from threads of ancient civilizations, Islamic dynasties, and European influences. To understand the Morocco of today, one must journey through the annals of its past.

Geographically, Morocco is a land of contrasts. Its northern coast meets the Mediterranean Sea, while the Atlantic Ocean kisses its western shores. The mighty Atlas Mountains dominate the center, offering breathtaking vistas and opportunities for adventure. To the south lies the vast Sahara Desert, a realm of shifting sands and nomadic traditions.

The story of Morocco's heritage begins in antiquity. Long before the Arab and Islamic influence, it was inhabited by Berber tribes, whose roots reach back thousands of years. These indigenous people, known for their resilience, have left an indelible mark on Moroccan culture and identity.

The Arab conquest in the 7th century brought Islam to Morocco, shaping its religious and architectural landscape. Magnificent mosques and madrasas, adorned with intricate tilework and calligraphy, stand as testaments to this enduring faith.

Morocco's history is also marked by dynastic rule. From the Idrisids to the Alawites, a series of dynasties have governed this land, each leaving its own imprint on the nation's character. The iconic city of Fes, with its labyrinthine medina, stands as a living testament to the architectural and intellectual achievements of the Merinid dynasty.

The colonial era saw Morocco under French and Spanish rule, which left a lasting impact on the nation's culture, language, and administration. Today, the influence of the French language and European architecture remains prominent, particularly in cities like Casablanca and Rabat.

Modern Morocco is a blend of tradition and progress. Its cities bustle with activity, and the economy thrives on agriculture, tourism, and industry. Yet, the heart of Moroccan identity lies in its ancient customs and rituals. The tantalizing aroma of tajine cooking in clay pots, the enchanting sound of traditional Gnawa music, and the intricate beauty of Moroccan carpets all speak to the nation's enduring traditions.

Morocco is also a land of linguistic diversity. While Arabic is the official language, the Berber language, Tamazight, persists in rural regions. French, a legacy of the colonial period, is widely spoken and serves as a bridge between Morocco and the Francophone world.

In the chapters that follow, we will delve deeper into Morocco's multifaceted identity. We will explore its geographical wonders, the diversity of its cities, its cuisine that tantalizes the taste buds, and the mesmerizing allure of its culture. As we embark on this journey through Morocco, we will uncover the layers of this enigmatic nation and reveal the tapestry of its rich heritage.

Geographical Diversity of Morocco

Morocco, a land of astonishing geographical diversity, unfolds like a grand tapestry of nature's wonders. From its pristine coastlines to its rugged mountain ranges and the sweeping sands of the Sahara Desert, Morocco's landscapes are a testament to the beauty and variety found within this North African gem.

Starting with its northern coastline, Morocco graces the Mediterranean Sea with picturesque beaches and charming coastal towns. Cities like Tangier, with its historical significance as the gateway to Africa and Europe, offer not only cultural richness but also stunning vistas of the sea. As you move south along the coast, you'll encounter cities like Casablanca, a thriving economic hub known for its modernity, and Essaouira, a coastal gem known for its tranquility and artistic flair.

Venturing inland, the landscape begins to transform as you approach the Atlas Mountains. These towering peaks dominate the central region of Morocco and provide a stark contrast to the coastal areas. The Atlas Mountains are divided into three ranges: the High Atlas, the Middle Atlas, and the Anti-Atlas. Each range has its unique character, from snow-capped peaks in the High Atlas to the lush forests of the Middle Atlas and the rugged terrain of the Anti-Atlas.

Marrakech, one of Morocco's most famous cities, lies at the foot of the High Atlas Mountains. This historic city is a true oasis in the midst of the arid landscape, with lush gardens and palm trees providing respite from the desert sun.

Heading southeast from the Atlas Mountains, you'll find yourself entering the vast Sahara Desert, one of the world's most iconic and inhospitable landscapes. The Sahara stretches across much of southern Morocco, where endless dunes of golden sand extend as far as the eye can see. This harsh yet mesmerizing environment is home to nomadic tribes and a unique ecosystem adapted to extreme conditions.

Morocco's interior regions are not just deserts; they also boast fertile oases, such as the Draa Valley and the Todra Gorge, where date palms flourish and agriculture thrives. These pockets of greenery are a testament to the resourcefulness of the Moroccan people in harnessing the precious waters of the region's rivers.

The country's geographical diversity extends further to its rich river valleys, including the Moulouya, Sebou, and Oum Er-Rbia rivers. These waterways have played a vital role in shaping Morocco's history and supporting its agriculture.

As we journey through Morocco's geographical tapestry, we will explore its natural beauty, the unique challenges posed by its diverse landscapes, and the ways in which the Moroccan people have adapted to and thrived in this remarkable country. From the coasts to the mountains and the deserts to the oases, Morocco's geographical diversity is an integral part of its identity and allure.

Early History and Ancient Civilizations

In the annals of time, Morocco's early history is a tapestry woven with threads of ancient civilizations, each contributing to the rich and diverse cultural mosaic that defines the nation today. The story of Morocco's early history is a journey through millennia, marked by the footsteps of Berbers, Phoenicians, Carthaginians, and Romans.

The earliest known inhabitants of the region we now call Morocco were the Berbers, an indigenous people whose presence can be traced back over 5,000 years. These resourceful and resilient nomadic tribes were skilled farmers and herders, adapting to the varying landscapes of the region. Their oral traditions, languages, and customs continue to shape the cultural identity of Morocco.

The Phoenicians, famed seafarers and traders, established settlements along Morocco's Mediterranean coast around 1100 BCE. The most notable of these was the ancient city of Lixus, known for its trade in precious metals and minerals. The influence of the Phoenicians on Moroccan culture was profound, introducing elements of maritime trade and early urbanization.

In the 6th century BCE, the Carthaginians, an ancient North African civilization, expanded their dominion into present-day Morocco. Carthage, their mighty city-state, established control over coastal areas and influenced local trade and governance. Carthaginian presence in Morocco was a precursor to the later Roman conquests in the region.

The Roman Empire, known for its vast territorial reach, extended its influence into Morocco in the 2nd century BCE. The Roman province of Mauretania Tingitana covered much of modern northern Morocco and was characterized by the construction of impressive cities like Volubilis and Banasa. Volubilis, in particular, stands as a well-preserved testament to Roman architectural and engineering prowess, featuring intricate mosaics, grand arches, and imposing columns.

The fall of the Roman Empire in the 5th century CE led to a period of instability in Morocco, with various Berber and Arab dynasties vying for control. It wasn't until the arrival of Islam in the 7th century CE that Morocco's cultural landscape underwent a profound transformation. The spread of Islam brought with it new architecture, art, and religious practices that would leave an enduring mark on the region.

The early history of Morocco is a story of migration, conquest, and cultural exchange. It is a tale of diverse civilizations converging on this North African land, leaving behind remnants of their existence in the form of archaeological treasures, language, and customs.

The Berbers: Indigenous People of Morocco

In the heart of Morocco's history lies a people whose roots in the land stretch back thousands of years—the Berbers. These indigenous inhabitants have been an integral part of Morocco's cultural landscape, shaping its traditions, languages, and customs with a rich tapestry of heritage that endures to this day.

The Berbers, known as the Imazighen or Amazigh in their own language, Tamazight, are a diverse group of ethnic communities spread across North Africa. Their presence in Morocco can be traced as far back as 3000 BCE, making them one of the oldest indigenous groups in the region. To understand the essence of Morocco, one must delve into the history and culture of the Berber people.

Throughout history, Berber society has been organized into various tribes and clans, each with its own unique customs and dialects. This tribal structure has enabled them to adapt and thrive in Morocco's varied landscapes, from the fertile plains to the mountainous regions to the deserts.

The Berbers have been resilient, mastering the art of survival in arid regions through sophisticated agricultural practices, including terraced farming and the cultivation of drought-resistant crops like barley and olives. Their intimate knowledge of the land and its resources has allowed them to flourish even in challenging environments. Language is a cornerstone of Berber identity, and the Tamazight language has a rich oral tradition, passed down through generations. It's a testament to their cultural continuity and resilience in the face of external influences. While Arabic has become the dominant language in modern Morocco, Tamazight remains a vital component of the nation's identity.

The Berbers' spiritual beliefs and practices have evolved over time. Traditionally animist, with reverence for nature and ancestral spirits, the arrival of Islam in the 7th century CE led to a blending of religious practices. Today, many Berbers practice a unique blend of Islamic and indigenous spiritual beliefs.

Berber craftsmanship and artistry are renowned, with a focus on intricate geometric designs and vivid colors. This artistic flair is evident in their traditional clothing, jewelry, and woven textiles, which are prized for their beauty and symbolism.

The Berbers have also played a pivotal role in Moroccan history. From the Berber dynasties that ruled Morocco, such as the Almoravids and Almohads, to their participation in various movements for independence, the Berber people have left an indelible mark on the nation's history.

In recent years, efforts have been made to preserve and promote Berber culture and language. Tamazight has gained official recognition, and Berber festivals and celebrations are celebrated nationwide. This recognition reflects the importance of the Berbers in shaping Morocco's national identity.

As we explore the Berbers and their profound influence on Morocco, we gain insight into a people whose enduring traditions and deep connection to the land have made them an integral part of the nation's rich and diverse heritage. Their story is a testament to the resilience of indigenous cultures and the dynamic interplay between tradition and modernity in Morocco.

Arab Influence and the Arrival of Islam

The arrival of Islam in Morocco marked a profound turning point in the nation's history, ushering in an era of religious transformation and cultural integration. This chapter delves into the Arab influence and the spread of Islam throughout Morocco, illuminating a pivotal period that has left an enduring impact on the nation.

Islam, one of the world's major monotheistic religions, first entered Morocco in the 7th century CE, following the rapid expansion of the Arab Empire. Led by Islamic conquerors, Arab armies swept across North Africa, bringing with them not only a new faith but also a new way of life.

The arrival of Islam in Morocco was not solely a religious transformation; it was also a catalyst for social and political change. Prior to the Arab conquest, Morocco was a land inhabited by Berber tribes with diverse belief systems and social structures. The spread of Islam gradually unified the region under a common religious framework.

The city of Tangier played a pivotal role in Morocco's early Islamic history. It was here, in the early 8th century, that Arab general Uqba ibn Nafi established one of the first Islamic garrisons in North Africa. This marked the beginning of the Arabization process in Morocco. One of the most significant aspects of Arab influence was the introduction of the Arabic language, which became the language of administration, religion, and culture. Arabic's prominence in Morocco persists to this day, as it is the nation's official language. The impact of Islam on Morocco's cultural landscape was profound. It brought with it architectural marvels like mosques and madrasas adorned with intricate tilework and calligraphy. These structures, such as the iconic Hassan II Mosque in Casablanca, stand as testaments to the enduring faith and architectural prowess of the Islamic civilization.

The religious and philosophical traditions of Islam enriched Morocco's intellectual life. The establishment of centers of learning, known as madrasas, became hubs of scholarship and education. Fes, in particular, became renowned as a center of Islamic learning, boasting one of the world's oldest universities, the University of Al Quaraouiyine, founded in 859 CE.

The spread of Islam also influenced Morocco's legal and ethical framework. Islamic law, or Sharia, became the basis for the nation's legal system, guiding matters of justice, family law, and personal conduct.

Morocco's geography played a crucial role in its early Islamic history. Its proximity to Spain and its location as a crossroads for trade between Africa and Europe contributed to the exchange of ideas, knowledge, and cultures.

The Berbers, while converting to Islam, also retained elements of their indigenous beliefs and practices, resulting in a unique blend of Islamic and traditional Berber customs that continue to shape Morocco's cultural landscape.

The Arab influence and the arrival of Islam in Morocco laid the foundation for a religious and cultural identity that endures to this day. It is a testament to the power of faith and the transformative influence of a new belief system on a diverse and dynamic society. In the chapters that follow, we will delve deeper into Morocco's historical journey, exploring the dynasties that ruled the land and the enduring traditions that have shaped the nation.

Dynasties of Morocco: From Idrisids to Alawites

Morocco's rich historical tapestry is interwoven with the legacies of dynastic rule, each dynasty leaving an indelible mark on the nation's identity and development. From the early days of the Idrisids to the enduring Alawite dynasty, the story of Morocco is a story of dynastic shifts, cultural evolution, and political resilience.

The Idrisid dynasty, founded in the late 8th century by Idris I, was the first to establish a centralized rule in Morocco. Idris I's leadership was marked by the foundation of Fes, one of Morocco's oldest and most culturally significant cities. The Idrisids were notable for their role in spreading Islam and creating a sense of unity among the diverse Berber tribes.

Following the decline of the Idrisid dynasty, Morocco experienced a period of fragmentation and conflict. It was during this time that the Almoravid dynasty emerged in the 11th century under the leadership of Abdallah ibn Yasin. The Almoravids' rule was characterized by their strict interpretation of Islamic law and their efforts to combat what they perceived as religious deviations. They expanded their empire beyond Morocco, reaching as far as Spain.

The Almohad dynasty succeeded the Almoravids in the 12th century. Under the leadership of Muhammad ibn Tumart, the Almohads sought to establish a more centralized and puritanical Islamic state. Their reign saw the construction of iconic architectural wonders, including the Koutoubia Mosque in Marrakech.

The Marinid dynasty, which followed in the 13th century, played a significant role in Morocco's cultural and intellectual development. They established Fes as a center of learning and culture, fostering the growth of universities and libraries.

The Wattasid dynasty, which succeeded the Marinids in the late 15th century, faced external pressures, particularly from Portuguese and Spanish forces. During this period, European powers began establishing footholds along Morocco's coast, leading to challenges for Moroccan sovereignty.

In the 17th century, the Saadi dynasty emerged, reuniting the country and expelling foreign powers. Their rule was characterized by a renewed sense of Moroccan identity and a resurgence of the arts and sciences.

However, the Saadi dynasty was supplanted by the Alawite dynasty in the late 17th century under the leadership of Moulay Ismail. The Alawites have remained the ruling dynasty in Morocco to the present day, marking one of the longest-standing royal dynasties in the world. Under Alawite rule, Morocco continued to evolve, experiencing periods of territorial expansion, modernization, and political reform.

Throughout these dynastic transitions, Morocco's cultural heritage thrived. Architectural marvels, intricate crafts, and vibrant traditions were shaped by the dynamic interplay of Berber, Arab, Islamic, and European influences. The Moroccan identity was forged through the centuries, blending the rich tapestry of its past into the vibrant nation we see today.

The dynasties of Morocco, from the Idrisids to the Alawites, are threads in the intricate fabric of Morocco's history. Their legacies have left an enduring mark on the nation's culture, religion, and political landscape, shaping Morocco into the unique and multifaceted nation it is today.

The French and Spanish Colonial Period

The French and Spanish colonial period in Morocco is a chapter in the nation's history marked by external influence, territorial struggles, and the enduring impact of European powers on Moroccan society. This era, which spanned from the late 19th century to the mid-20th century, brought profound changes to Morocco's political, economic, and cultural landscape.

The 19th century saw Morocco facing increasing pressure from European colonial powers eager to expand their influence in North Africa. France and Spain, in particular, sought footholds in Morocco due to its strategic location and economic potential. In 1904, France and the United Kingdom signed the Entente Cordiale, which effectively divided Morocco into French and Spanish zones of influence.

The Treaty of Fez in 1912 formalized these divisions, making Morocco a French and Spanish protectorate. Under this arrangement, Morocco retained its sovereignty in name but was, in reality, under the control of the European powers. Each colonial power governed its respective zone, with the French zone covering the majority of the country, including major cities like Casablanca and Rabat, while the Spanish zone encompassed areas in the north.

The colonial period brought significant changes to Moroccan society. The French and Spanish introduced modern infrastructure, such as railways, roads, and ports, which facilitated the movement of goods and people. This period also witnessed the expansion of education, with the establishment of schools and institutions that blended European and Moroccan curricula.

Economically, the colonial powers sought to exploit Morocco's resources. French and Spanish companies invested in mining, agriculture, and manufacturing, which led to the development of Morocco's economy but also resulted in the extraction of resources for the benefit of the colonizers.

The colonial era was marked by resistance from the Moroccan population, who viewed the European presence as a threat to their sovereignty and way of life. This resistance culminated in the Rif War (1920-1927), a conflict between the Spanish colonial forces and Berber tribes in the Rif region. The war had a profound impact on Moroccan society and left a legacy of resistance and nationalism.

The French and Spanish colonial period also witnessed cultural interactions and exchanges. Moroccan artists and intellectuals engaged with European ideas, leading to the emergence of modern Moroccan literature and art. However, this period was also marked by efforts to suppress and control indigenous culture and traditions.

World War II had a significant impact on Morocco's colonial status. In 1942, during the war, the French government-in-exile, led by Charles de Gaulle, declared Morocco's independence from Vichy France, the collaborationist regime. After the war, the international community, including the United Nations, called for the decolonization of Morocco.

In 1956, Morocco gained its independence from France and Spain, ending the colonial period. Sultan Mohammed V became the king of Morocco, marking a new era for the nation.

The French and Spanish colonial period in Morocco was a time of significant change and challenge. It left a complex legacy of modernization, resistance, cultural exchange, and, ultimately, the path to independence. Morocco's struggle for sovereignty and self-determination during this period played a crucial role in shaping the nation's identity and its place in the modern world.

Modern Morocco: Independence and Governance

The post-colonial era marked a significant turning point in Morocco's history, as the nation embarked on a journey toward independence and self-governance. This chapter explores the complexities of modern Morocco, tracing its path from colonial rule to the establishment of a constitutional monarchy and its ongoing efforts to balance tradition with modernity.

In 1956, Morocco gained its independence from French and Spanish colonial rule. King Mohammed V, who had become the symbol of resistance against the colonial powers, returned to lead the nation. His reign marked the beginning of a new era characterized by the restoration of Moroccan sovereignty and the pursuit of a modern, independent state.

Under King Mohammed V and later his son, King Hassan II, Morocco faced numerous challenges. One of the most significant was the consolidation of power and the establishment of a stable government. In 1962, Morocco adopted a new constitution, which laid the groundwork for a constitutional monarchy with a parliamentary system. This marked a shift from absolute monarchy to a more representative form of governance.

During King Hassan II's rule, Morocco saw both economic development and political turbulence. The monarchy played a central role in the nation's politics, and the government faced opposition from various political and social groups seeking greater democratic reforms. The 1960s and 1970s witnessed a series of protests and political unrest.

One of the most significant events during this period was the Green March of 1975, during which King Hassan II called on Moroccans to peacefully reclaim the disputed territory of Western Sahara. This led to the incorporation of the region into Morocco, although the issue remains a subject of international dispute to this day.

In the late 1990s, King Mohammed VI ascended to the throne, ushering in a period of gradual political and social reform. The new king introduced constitutional amendments in 1996 and 2011, strengthening the powers of elected officials and promoting human rights. Morocco's political landscape evolved with the establishment of multiparty elections and greater civil liberties.

Economically, Morocco embarked on a path of liberalization and diversification. The nation's economy expanded, driven by sectors such as agriculture, tourism, and manufacturing. Infrastructure development continued, with investments in transportation and energy.

Morocco's role in regional and international affairs also grew. The nation became a key player in diplomacy and peacekeeping efforts in North Africa and the Middle East. Its strategic location as a bridge between Africa and Europe made it an important partner for trade and diplomacy.

Culturally, Morocco's diverse heritage continued to thrive. The nation's unique blend of Berber, Arab, Islamic, and European influences was celebrated through art, music, literature, and festivals. The preservation of traditional customs, such as mint tea ceremonies and colorful local markets, coexisted with the embrace of modernity.

Challenges persist in modern Morocco, including economic disparities, youth unemployment, and political reforms. However, the nation's commitment to democratic principles, its efforts to improve human rights, and its engagement with the international community continue to shape its path forward.

As we examine modern Morocco, we witness a nation that has navigated the complexities of history, governance, and cultural identity. It is a nation that continues to evolve, seeking a balance between tradition and progress as it defines its place in the modern world.

Moroccan Wildlife and Ecological Wonders

Morocco's natural landscapes are a treasure trove of biodiversity, from the windswept Sahara Desert to the lush Atlas Mountains and the pristine coastal areas along the Mediterranean and Atlantic. In this chapter, we explore the remarkable wildlife and ecological wonders that grace this North African nation.

The Sahara Desert, one of the world's most iconic deserts, occupies a vast portion of southern Morocco. Despite its arid reputation, the Sahara is home to a surprising array of wildlife adapted to its extreme conditions. Dromedary camels are synonymous with the desert, serving as vital means of transportation for nomadic communities. Desert foxes, desert hedgehogs, and fennec foxes are among the nocturnal inhabitants, while various species of desert birds, such as sandgrouse and falcons, thrive in this challenging environment.

Heading north from the Sahara, Morocco's Atlas Mountains provide a stark contrast in terms of climate and habitat. The High Atlas, Middle Atlas, and Anti-Atlas ranges offer diverse ecosystems, from snow-capped peaks to fertile valleys and dense cedar forests. These mountains are home to the endangered Barbary macaque, a primate species unique to North Africa. Birdwatchers also find solace in the Atlas Mountains, with golden eagles, Egyptian vultures, and Atlas mountain finches gracing the skies.

Morocco's forests are a sanctuary for diverse flora and fauna. The cork oak forests of the Middle Atlas are not only a source of cork production but also habitat for Barbary deer, wild boars, and a variety of bird species. Cedar forests in the High Atlas provide shelter for the Barbary macaque and the elusive North African leopard, though sightings of the latter are exceedingly rare.

Wetlands play a crucial role in Morocco's ecosystem, serving as vital stopover points for migratory birds. The Souss-Massa National Park, situated along the Atlantic coast, is a designated Ramsar site and a haven for birdwatchers. Flamingos, herons, and avocets are just a few of the many avian species that call these wetlands home.

Morocco's coastline, stretching along both the Mediterranean and Atlantic, is teeming with marine life. The waters off the coast are frequented by dolphins, including the common dolphin and bottlenose dolphin, as well as migratory whales such as humpback whales. Morocco's rich fishing grounds are also home to a variety of fish species, including sardines and swordfish.

In the southeast, Morocco shares a border with Algeria, where the Tassili n'Ajjer plateau boasts prehistoric rock art and landscapes that reveal the area's ancient history. This region is a testament to the connection between Morocco's natural wonders and its cultural heritage.

Efforts to conserve Morocco's ecological wonders are ongoing, with national parks and protected areas playing a pivotal role. The High Atlas Foundation and other organizations are working to preserve and restore Morocco's landscapes, ensuring that these ecological wonders continue to thrive for generations to come.

Morocco's wildlife and ecological diversity are a testament to the nation's unique geography and its commitment to conservation. From the desert to the mountains, wetlands to the coast, Morocco's natural wonders inspire awe and appreciation for the delicate balance of life in this remarkable North African nation.

A Culinary Journey Through Moroccan Cuisine

Moroccan cuisine is a tantalizing fusion of flavors, a reflection of the nation's rich history, diverse culture, and the bountiful offerings of its landscapes. This chapter invites you on a sensory adventure through the vibrant and aromatic world of Moroccan food, where spices, tradition, and innovation converge to create a culinary tapestry that delights the palate.

At the heart of Moroccan cuisine lies the iconic tagine, a slow-cooked stew prepared in a distinctive conical clay pot. Tagines can be made with a variety of ingredients, such as tender lamb, chicken, or fish, combined with an assortment of vegetables and a medley of spices, including cumin, coriander, and saffron. The result is a flavorful and fragrant dish that embodies the essence of Moroccan cooking.

Couscous, often referred to as the national dish of Morocco, is another cornerstone of Moroccan cuisine. This tiny grain, made from semolina wheat, is steamed to perfection and served with an array of savory toppings, such as tender meat, vegetables, and aromatic sauces. Couscous is a staple on Moroccan dinner tables, and its preparation is a labor of love, often involving hours of steaming and fluffing.

Harira, a hearty soup often enjoyed during Ramadan and special occasions, is a beloved Moroccan classic. This tomato-based soup is brimming with lentils, chickpeas, herbs, and spices, creating a nourishing and comforting dish. It's traditionally accompanied by dates and sweet pastries, creating a perfect balance of flavors. The streets of Morocco come alive with the enticing aroma of street food vendors.

One cannot resist the sizzle of meat skewers, known as brochettes, or the savory embrace of a warm and fluffy Moroccan sandwich, bocadillos. These street treats are a testament to Morocco's vibrant street food culture, where locals and tourists alike indulge in the flavors of the souks.

Moroccan cuisine also boasts an array of delectable sweets. From the iconic pastilla, a flaky pastry filled with sweet and savory delights, to the honey-soaked delights of baklava and the rich, almond-studded layers of pastries like m'hanncha, Morocco's dessert offerings are a true testament to the nation's culinary artistry.

Mint tea, or "atay," is the national drink of Morocco and holds a special place in Moroccan culture. This refreshing blend of green tea, fresh mint leaves, and sugar is a symbol of hospitality and tradition. The tea is typically poured with great care from a height to create a frothy top, and it is enjoyed throughout the day.

Morocco's culinary traditions are deeply rooted in its diverse culture and history. Berber, Arab, and Moorish influences have all contributed to the complexity and depth of Moroccan flavors. The country's geographical diversity, from the fertile plains to the coastal regions and the arid deserts, has given rise to a wide range of ingredients and cooking techniques.

Exploring Moroccan cuisine is not just about tasting exquisite dishes; it's also a journey through the heart of Moroccan culture and hospitality. Food in Morocco is not merely sustenance; it's a celebration of life, a reflection of history, and a source of pride for the Moroccan people. As you embark on this culinary journey, you'll discover the magic of Moroccan cuisine, where every bite tells a story and every meal is a feast for the senses.

The Exquisite World of Moroccan Tea

Morocco's cultural identity is intrinsically linked to its love affair with tea. When you think of Moroccan hospitality, vibrant bazaars, or serene desert oases, a steaming glass of mint tea, known as "atay," is never far from the imagination. This chapter takes you on a delightful journey through the intricate and cherished world of Moroccan tea.

Moroccan tea is not merely a beverage; it's a ritual, a gesture of warmth and hospitality that transcends cultural and linguistic boundaries. This aromatic elixir is deeply ingrained in Moroccan culture, and its preparation and consumption are steeped in tradition.

Green tea forms the foundation of Moroccan tea. The Chinese gunpowder green tea variety is most commonly used, known for its robust flavor and ability to withstand the addition of mint and sugar. Fresh sprigs of spearmint, or "nana," are the essential aromatic companion, adding a burst of refreshing flavor and fragrance.

The preparation of Moroccan tea is an art form, often performed with great flair and attention to detail. To start, loose tea leaves are steeped in hot water, allowing the flavors to bloom and infuse. Next, generous handfuls of fresh mint leaves are added, giving the tea its signature aroma. Finally, an ample amount of sugar, usually in the form of sugar cubes or a sugar cone, is added to balance the herbal bitterness of the tea. But what truly sets Moroccan tea apart is the pouring technique. The tea is poured from a height, often held aloft by the server's outstretched arm, into small, ornate glasses. This graceful act not only cools the tea slightly but also creates a frothy layer on top, enhancing the visual and sensory experience. Tea in Morocco is not just a daily ritual; it's a symbol of hospitality and connection. Moroccan hosts take pride in offering guests a glass of tea, and it's customary to share multiple rounds during social gatherings. The first glass is said to be as bitter as death, the second as strong as love, and the third as soothing as marriage, a poetic expression of the evolving flavors and emotions experienced while savoring Moroccan tea.

Moroccan tea transcends borders and has become a global sensation, appreciated for its invigorating flavors and aromatic charm. Cafes and tea houses in Morocco and around the world serve this beloved beverage, creating spaces for people to gather, converse, and appreciate the simple pleasure of sharing a cup of tea.

Tea has also played a role in Moroccan history. It's said that tea was introduced to Morocco by British merchants in the 18th century, and its popularity quickly spread. Today, Morocco ranks among the top tea consumers globally, and its tea-drinking culture continues to thrive.

Beyond its cultural significance, Moroccan tea has a place in traditional medicine. Mint tea is often used as a natural remedy for digestive ailments, and the combination of green tea and mint is believed to have various health benefits.

In the enchanting world of Moroccan tea, every sip is an invitation to savor life's simple pleasures and to connect with the heart of Moroccan culture. Whether enjoyed in a bustling Marrakech market, a tranquil desert camp, or the comfort of your own home, Moroccan tea is an embodiment of the country's warmth, tradition, and enduring love for the art of hospitality.

Tangier - Gateway to Africa and Europe

Tangier, a city steeped in history and perched at the crossroads of two continents, serves as a captivating gateway between Africa and Europe. Its unique position on the northern tip of Morocco, overlooking the Strait of Gibraltar, has made it a nexus of culture, commerce, and intrigue for centuries.

The history of Tangier is a tapestry woven with threads from various civilizations. Phoenician traders established a settlement here in the 5th century BCE, followed by successive waves of influence from Carthaginians, Romans, Vandals, Byzantines, and Arab conquerors. It was the Arab rulers who transformed Tangier into a bustling port city and a hub for trade between North Africa and the Mediterranean.

Throughout the medieval period, Tangier exchanged hands multiple times, with European powers vying for control. In 1471, it became part of the Portuguese Empire, marking the start of European colonial rule in the region. The Portuguese held Tangier until 1661 when it was handed over to England as part of the dowry of Catherine of Braganza upon her marriage to King Charles II.

However, Tangier's strategic importance in controlling the entrance to the Mediterranean led to conflict and competition among European powers. In 1684, England abandoned Tangier, and it was subsequently claimed by various countries, including Spain and France. Ultimately, in 1923, Tangier became an international zone under the administration of multiple nations, symbolizing its unique status as an international meeting point.

This international era of Tangier was characterized by cultural exchange and a cosmopolitan atmosphere. Writers, artists, and diplomats flocked to the city, drawn by its blend of European, Arab, and Berber influences. It was during this time that Tangier gained a reputation for intrigue and espionage, fueling the imaginations of authors like Paul Bowles and William S. Burroughs, who called the city home.

In 1956, Tangier returned to Moroccan sovereignty when Morocco gained its independence from colonial rule. The city remained a symbol of international cooperation and cultural diversity. Today, it continues to be a melting pot of cultures, with its medina (old town) a UNESCO World Heritage Site, preserving centuries of history and architecture.

Tangier's strategic location has also made it a vital transportation hub. Ferries and ships connect Tangier to Spain, making it the main gateway for travelers between Africa and Europe. The city is a bustling port, with its new Tanger-Med port complex being one of the largest in Africa and playing a pivotal role in international trade.

Tourism is a significant part of Tangier's modern identity. Visitors are drawn to its historic medina, bustling markets, and picturesque coastline. The American Legation Museum, housed in the former U.S. consulate, stands as a testament to the city's international heritage. The Kasbah, with its narrow winding streets and stunning views, is a must-visit for anyone exploring Tangier.

Tangier's unique position as the "Gateway to Africa and Europe" continues to shape its identity and its role in the modern world. It's a city that has always been a meeting point for cultures, a place where histories collide, and where the promise of new beginnings and adventures beckons travelers from both sides of the Strait of Gibraltar.

Casablanca - Morocco's Economic Hub

Casablanca, a name that resonates with romance and intrigue thanks to the iconic film of the same name, is also Morocco's economic powerhouse. This bustling metropolis, with its modern skyline and vibrant streets, serves as the beating heart of Morocco's commerce, industry, and finance.

Situated along the country's Atlantic coastline, Casablanca is the largest city in Morocco and one of the largest in Africa. Its strategic location has historically made it a vital port city, facilitating trade between Morocco, Europe, and the rest of the world. The Port of Casablanca is one of the largest and busiest on the continent, handling a significant portion of Morocco's imports and exports.

The city's economic significance dates back to the French colonial period when it underwent extensive urban development. This laid the foundation for the modern infrastructure that exists today. Casablanca's wide boulevards, European-inspired architecture, and modern amenities stand in contrast to the historic medinas of other Moroccan cities.

One of Casablanca's key economic drivers is its thriving manufacturing sector. The city is home to numerous industrial zones, where a wide range of products, from textiles to electronics, are produced for both domestic consumption and export. This has contributed significantly to Morocco's economic growth.

Casablanca is also a financial hub, hosting the Casablanca Stock Exchange and the headquarters of many national and international banks and financial institutions. The city plays a central role in Morocco's banking and finance sector, facilitating investment and economic development.

Morocco's commitment to modernization and infrastructure development is evident in Casablanca. The city boasts a well-connected transportation network, including an extensive tram system, a modern airport, and a high-speed train connection to other major cities like Rabat and Tangier. These investments have enhanced Casablanca's role as a regional and international business hub.

The Mohammed V International Airport, located in the vicinity of Casablanca, is the busiest in Morocco, serving as a major gateway for both business and leisure travelers. Its strategic location makes it a convenient entry point for those exploring Morocco's diverse landscapes and rich culture.

The city's economic influence extends beyond its borders. The Casablanca-Settat region, of which Casablanca is the capital, contributes significantly to Morocco's overall GDP. The region encompasses numerous industrial zones, agricultural areas, and thriving urban centers.

While Casablanca is often associated with commerce and industry, it is also a city of culture and creativity. Its vibrant arts scene, modern galleries, and dynamic music scene are testament to its cultural richness. The Hassan II Mosque, one of the largest mosques in the world, stands as an architectural marvel and a symbol of Morocco's spiritual heritage.

Casablanca's economic dynamism has led to a diverse and multicultural population. People from various regions of Morocco and around the world come to the city in pursuit of economic opportunities. This cultural diversity enriches the city's social fabric, cuisine, and daily life.

As we explore Casablanca's role as Morocco's economic hub, we uncover a city that embodies the nation's commitment to progress and development. It's a place where tradition and modernity coexist, where the allure of business and innovation meets the charm of Moroccan hospitality. In the heart of Casablanca, Morocco's economic aspirations find their vibrant and thriving home.

Marrakech - The Red City of History and Magic

Marrakech, often referred to as the "Red City" due to the distinctive hue of its ancient walls, is a place where history and magic intertwine to create an unforgettable experience. Located in the heart of Morocco, Marrakech is a city that has captivated travelers for centuries with its vibrant souks, grand palaces, and enchanting gardens.

The history of Marrakech is a tapestry woven with threads from Berber, Arab, and Andalusian influences. Founded in 1070 by the Almoravid dynasty, the city served as the capital of their empire, marking the beginning of Marrakech's historical significance. Over the centuries, it witnessed the rise and fall of various dynasties, including the Almohads and the Saadian rulers.

One of Marrakech's most iconic landmarks is the Koutoubia Mosque, an exquisite example of Almohad architecture. Its towering minaret, adorned with intricate geometric patterns, is a symbol of the city and a testament to the skilled craftsmanship of its builders.

The heart of Marrakech lies within the medina, a UNESCO World Heritage Site. This labyrinthine old town is a sensory overload, where narrow winding streets lead to bustling souks filled with colorful textiles, fragrant spices, and handcrafted treasures. The medina is home to a rich tapestry of artisans, from silversmiths and weavers to woodcarvers and leather craftsmen, each preserving and passing down their traditional skills.

Jemaa el-Fnaa, the main square in Marrakech, is a place of ceaseless energy and spectacle. By day, it's a bustling market where vendors hawk their wares, and snake charmers mesmerize onlookers. As the sun sets, the square transforms into an open-air theater, with storytellers, musicians, and street food vendors creating a vibrant atmosphere that's uniquely Marrakech.

Marrakech's historic palaces and gardens offer a glimpse into its regal past. The Bahia Palace, with its intricate mosaics and lush courtyards, is a testament to Moroccan architecture and the opulence of the late 19th century. The Saadian Tombs, discovered in the early 20th century, reveal beautifully preserved mausoleums dating back to the 16th century.

The Majorelle Garden, a creation of French painter Jacques Majorelle, is a tranquil oasis in the heart of the city. Its vibrant blue buildings, lush gardens, and collection of exotic plants offer a serene escape from the bustling streets.

Marrakech's cuisine is a fusion of flavors and traditions. The city's famous tagines, fragrant with spices and slow-cooked tenderness, are a culinary delight. Street food stalls offer tantalizing treats like grilled kebabs, savory pastries, and freshly squeezed orange juice. And of course, no visit to Marrakech is complete without savoring a glass of sweet mint tea.

Marrakech has also become a cultural hub, with art galleries, music festivals, and fashion boutiques showcasing the city's creative spirit. The city's unique blend of tradition and modernity is reflected in its vibrant arts scene, which continues to evolve.

As you explore Marrakech, you'll find that it's a city where time seems to stand still and yet is constantly evolving. Its history, culture, and enchantment are bound to leave an indelible mark on your memory. In the heart of the Red City, the past and the present coalesce to create an experience that is nothing short of magical.

Fes - The Spiritual and Cultural Heart

Fes, a city of profound spiritual significance and unparalleled cultural richness, occupies a special place in the heart of Morocco. As one of the country's oldest imperial cities, Fes has been a center of scholarship, spirituality, and craftsmanship for centuries, earning it the title of "The Spiritual and Cultural Heart."

Fes' history traces back over a thousand years, with its origins dating to the 8th century when it was founded by the Idrisid dynasty. The city served as the capital of Morocco during various dynasties, including the Almoravids and the Merinids. Its illustrious past is visible in every corner of the city, from its ancient walls to its meticulously preserved historic medina.

At the heart of Fes lies the medina, a UNESCO World Heritage Site and one of the world's largest car-free urban areas. The medina is a labyrinth of narrow alleyways, stunning architecture, and bustling souks where artisans practice traditional crafts passed down through generations. Fes is renowned for its intricate tilework, woodcarving, and leatherwork, which continue to flourish in the city's workshops.

The University of Al Quaraouiyine, founded in 859 CE, holds the distinction of being the world's oldest continually operating degree-granting university. It has been a center of Islamic scholarship for over a millennium, attracting students and scholars from across the Islamic world. The university's ancient library contains a treasure trove of manuscripts, some dating back to the 9th century.

Fes is also a city of spiritual significance, with numerous mosques, madrasas, and religious sites that reflect its deep-rooted Islamic heritage. The Bou Inania Madrasa, an architectural masterpiece, stands as a testament to the city's commitment to religious education and scholarship. The city's many mosques, including the grand Karaouine Mosque, offer places of contemplation and worship for both residents and visitors.

The souks of Fes are a sensory delight, where the scent of spices, the vibrant colors of textiles, and the rhythmic sounds of artisans at work create an immersive experience. Shoppers can browse a myriad of goods, from traditional carpets and ceramics to fragrant spices and intricate jewelry.

Fes is also known for its culinary delights. The city's cuisine is a tantalizing fusion of flavors, with dishes like the savory pastilla, tender tagines, and aromatic couscous gracing the tables of local homes and restaurants. The medina's food stalls offer a wide range of street food, allowing visitors to savor Moroccan delicacies like harira soup and freshly baked bread.

The city's annual Festival of World Sacred Music, held in the enchanting Bab Makina Palace, brings together musicians and artists from around the world to celebrate the universal language of music and spirituality. This festival is a testament to Fes' role as a bridge between cultures and traditions.

Fes is a living testament to Morocco's rich history, vibrant culture, and enduring traditions. Its medina, a time capsule of the past, continues to thrive as a center of craftsmanship and learning. The city's spiritual heritage and artistic legacy have left an indelible mark on Moroccan identity, making Fes a place where the past and present harmoniously coexist, and where every step you take reveals a new layer of its captivating history and culture.

Rabat - The Capital of Morocco

Rabat, Morocco's capital city, stands as a testament to the nation's history, culture, and modernity. Nestled along the Atlantic coast, Rabat's role as the political and administrative center of Morocco is complemented by its rich heritage, vibrant cultural scene, and the harmonious coexistence of tradition and progress.

While Rabat may not be as well-known internationally as some of Morocco's other cities, such as Marrakech or Casablanca, it plays a pivotal role in the country's governance. The decision to move the capital from Fez to Rabat in the 12th century marked the city's emergence as a center of political power and influence.

One of Rabat's most iconic landmarks is the Royal Palace, the official residence of the Moroccan monarch. While the palace itself is not open to the public, the grand entrance and ornate gates are a testament to Morocco's monarchy and the city's role as the seat of government.

The historic medina of Rabat, a UNESCO World Heritage Site, offers a glimpse into the city's rich past. Its narrow streets, bustling markets, and ancient architecture harken back to centuries of Berber, Arab, and Andalusian influence. Visitors can explore the vibrant Kasbah of the Udayas, a picturesque fortress overlooking the Atlantic Ocean, with its whitewashed walls and blue accents.

Rabat's modernity is evident in its well-planned streets, modern infrastructure, and vibrant cultural institutions. The Mohammed V Mausoleum, a magnificent structure that houses the tombs of King Mohammed V and King Hassan II, is a testament to Morocco's contemporary architecture and the reverence for its past rulers.

The city is also home to the prestigious Mohammed V University, one of Morocco's leading institutions of higher education. Rabat's educational and research facilities contribute significantly to the nation's intellectual and cultural growth.

Rabat's cultural scene is thriving, with museums like the Museum of Moroccan Contemporary Art and the National Archaeological Museum showcasing the country's artistic and historical treasures. The city's theaters, galleries, and music venues offer a platform for artists and performers to express themselves.

The tranquil Andalusian Gardens in Rabat are a green oasis amidst the urban landscape. These beautifully landscaped gardens provide a serene retreat for both residents and visitors, a place to escape the bustle of the city and enjoy moments of reflection.

Rabat's coastal location along the Atlantic Ocean adds to its charm. The city's beaches, including Plage de Rabat and Plage de Salé, provide opportunities for relaxation and water sports. The Bouregreg River, which separates Rabat from the neighboring city of Salé, is adorned with picturesque bridges and promenades.

As the political heart of Morocco, Rabat plays a critical role in shaping the nation's policies and direction. It is a city of diplomacy and international relations, with numerous embassies and international organizations calling it home.

Rabat's blend of tradition and modernity, its historical significance, and its role as the administrative capital make it a city that embodies Morocco's spirit of progress while honoring its rich cultural heritage. In Rabat, every street, every monument, and every institution tells a story of a nation at the crossroads of tradition and innovation, making it a city that is both the present and the future of Morocco.

Meknes - A Hidden Gem of Imperial Cities

Nestled amidst the rolling hills of northern Morocco, Meknes is a city that often escapes the limelight but deserves recognition as one of Morocco's hidden gems among the imperial cities. Founded in the 9th century, Meknes holds a rich history, grand architecture, and a unique blend of cultures that beckon travelers seeking to explore Morocco's past and present.

Meknes' imperial history is closely intertwined with that of Morocco. It was Sultan Moulay Ismail, who ruled from the late 17th century to the early 18th century, who elevated Meknes to its imperial status. His vision was grand, and his ambition led to the construction of the vast imperial city that stands today. The grandeur of Meknes is most evident in the monumental Bab Mansour, a massive gate that serves as the entrance to the city. Its ornate decoration, intricate tilework, and sheer size are a testament to the might and ambition of Sultan Moulay Ismail. The gate is often considered one of the most beautiful in Morocco.

Within Meknes, the Heri es-Souani granaries and stables are a testament to the scale of Moulay Ismail's vision. These enormous structures were designed to store grain and house thousands of horses. Their impressive architecture and vast dimensions are a reminder of the sultan's ambition to create a grand imperial capital. Meknes is also home to the Mausoleum of Moulay Ismail, where the sultan himself is laid to rest. The mausoleum is a sacred site, and its serene courtyard and beautiful tilework make it a place of reverence and tranquility. The medina of Meknes, a UNESCO World Heritage Site, is a charming labyrinth of narrow streets, bustling souks, and traditional Moroccan architecture. It offers a more relaxed and less crowded alternative to the medinas of cities like Marrakech and Fes, making it an ideal place for leisurely exploration and shopping.

While Meknes may be smaller than some of Morocco's other imperial cities, it is no less significant in terms of its cultural heritage. The city is known for its rich Berber traditions and the unique blend of Arab and Berber cultures that defines its character. This cultural diversity is evident in the city's cuisine, music, and daily life.

Meknes also serves as a gateway to the nearby Roman ruins of Volubilis, another UNESCO World Heritage Site. These ancient ruins, with their well-preserved mosaics and architectural remnants, offer a glimpse into Morocco's Roman past and are a must-visit for history enthusiasts.

The city's annual Meknes International Festival of Sacred Music celebrates Morocco's cultural diversity and the spiritual significance of music. It attracts musicians and visitors from around the world, adding a vibrant and international dimension to Meknes' cultural scene.

In Meknes, history and heritage are interwoven with the rhythms of daily life. It's a city where the echoes of imperial grandeur coexist with the simplicity of traditional markets and the warmth of its people. Meknes may be a hidden gem among Morocco's imperial cities, but its allure lies in its authenticity and the opportunity it offers to uncover the lesser-known facets of Morocco's rich cultural tapestry.

Chefchaouen - The Blue Pearl of Morocco

Tucked away in the Rif Mountains of northern Morocco, Chefchaouen, often referred to as the "Blue Pearl," is a town that seems plucked from a dream. With its stunning blue-painted buildings, winding cobblestone streets, and a tranquil mountain backdrop, Chefchaouen is a place of unique beauty and serenity.

The story of Chefchaouen's distinctive blue palette dates back to the 15th century when Jewish refugees settled in the town, escaping the Spanish Inquisition. The tradition of painting buildings blue is believed to have been brought by the Jewish community, as blue is a color that represents the sky and heaven in Judaism, symbolizing a connection to the divine.

Over the centuries, the blue tradition continued and expanded, covering walls, alleyways, and even doorways in shades of blue ranging from pale pastels to deep indigos. Today, this sea of blue is a defining feature of Chefchaouen and sets it apart from other Moroccan towns.

The calming effect of the blue surroundings is immediately evident as you wander through Chefchaouen's streets. The town's medina is a labyrinth of narrow passages and inviting courtyards, each one offering a new shade of blue to discover. It's a place where you can lose yourself in the enchanting play of light and color.

Chefchaouen is not just visually stunning; it's also a place of cultural richness. The town's history and traditions have been preserved and passed down through generations. The Andalusian influence is evident in the architecture, with intricate tilework, arches, and fountains adorning the buildings.

The Plaza Uta el-Hammam, the main square of Chefchaouen, is a hub of activity and a gathering place for locals and visitors alike. Cafes line the square, providing the perfect spot to sip Moroccan mint tea and people-watch. The square is also home to the Grand Mosque and the Kasbah, a fortress that now houses a museum showcasing the history and culture of the region.

Chefchaouen's natural surroundings are equally breathtaking. The Rif Mountains offer opportunities for hiking, with trails leading to panoramic viewpoints that overlook the town and surrounding valleys. The Akchour Waterfalls, a short drive from Chefchaouen, are a refreshing oasis nestled in the rugged landscape.

The town's laid-back atmosphere and welcoming residents make it a destination where you can truly unwind and connect with Moroccan culture. It's not uncommon to encounter friendly locals who are eager to share stories, invite you for tea, or offer insights into their way of life.

Chefchaouen's reputation as a hidden gem has grown over the years, attracting travelers seeking a quieter, more serene Moroccan experience. While it may not have the bustling markets or grand palaces of some other Moroccan cities, it offers a unique blend of natural beauty, cultural authenticity, and artistic charm.

In Chefchaouen, the color blue isn't just a pigment on walls; it's a reflection of the town's spirit—calm, inviting, and vibrant in its own way. As you explore the winding blue streets and immerse yourself in the tranquil ambiance of Chefchaouen, you'll discover that this "Blue Pearl" is a place where beauty and serenity come together in a truly enchanting way.

Essaouira - A Coastal Gem of Tranquility

On the western coast of Morocco, where the Atlantic Ocean meets the African continent, lies Essaouira, a coastal gem of tranquility that beckons travelers seeking respite from the bustling cities and a taste of Moroccan seaside charm. This picturesque town, with its distinctive blue boats, fortified medina, and windswept beaches, is a place where history, culture, and natural beauty intertwine.

Essaouira's roots trace back to the 18th century when it was established by Sultan Mohammed III as a strategic port city. The city's medina, a UNESCO World Heritage Site, boasts an exceptional blend of European military architecture and Moroccan aesthetics. The imposing seafront ramparts, complete with cannons that once defended against pirates, provide stunning views of the crashing waves and the horizon.

One of Essaouira's most iconic features is its blue fishing boats, which line the bustling port. These boats, adorned with vibrant blue hues, create a striking contrast against the white-washed buildings of the medina. The fishing industry remains a vital part of Essaouira's identity, and you can witness the daily catch being brought ashore and sold at the bustling fish market.

The medina's labyrinthine streets are a joy to explore. Unlike the chaotic markets of other Moroccan cities, Essaouira's souks exude a relaxed atmosphere. Artisans craft intricate woodwork, jewelry, and textiles, and you can watch skilled hands at work in small workshops tucked away in the medina's corners.

The city's artistic heritage is celebrated at the Essaouira-Mogador Festival, an annual event that brings together musicians, artists, and performers from Morocco and beyond. The festival's diverse program showcases the rich cultural tapestry of the region and adds a vibrant rhythm to the town's laid-back ambiance.

Essaouira's coastal location makes it a haven for water sports enthusiasts. The strong and consistent trade winds that sweep across the Atlantic have earned it the nickname "Windy City of Africa." Kite surfing and windsurfing are popular activities, attracting enthusiasts from around the world.

The wide sandy beaches of Essaouira offer the perfect setting for relaxation. You can bask in the sun, take a leisurely stroll along the shore, or even enjoy camel rides along the beach, taking in the dramatic coastal scenery.

The historic medina is a treasure trove of architectural gems. The Skala de la Ville, a sea-facing bastion, offers stunning panoramic views and a glimpse into the city's maritime history. The Moulay Hassan Square is a hub of activity, with cafes and restaurants where you can savor fresh seafood and local cuisine while watching the world go by.

Essaouira's mellowness and charm extend to its welcoming residents. The town's mix of Berber, Arab, and European influences has shaped a unique local culture characterized by warmth and hospitality. It's not uncommon to strike up conversations with locals eager to share their stories and insights.

As the sun sets over Essaouira, painting the sky in hues of orange and pink, you'll find that this coastal gem exudes a sense of tranquility that is both captivating and rejuvenating. Whether you're exploring its historic medina, savoring fresh seafood, or simply lounging on its windswept beaches, Essaouira is a place where you can unwind, connect with nature, and embrace the serene beauty of Morocco's Atlantic coast.

Sahara Desert - Mysteries of the Dunes

The Sahara Desert, a vast expanse of endless sand dunes and shifting landscapes, stands as one of the world's most enigmatic and awe-inspiring natural wonders. Its name alone conjures images of a harsh and unforgiving environment, yet beneath its scorching surface lies a world of intrigue and mystique.

Spanning over 3.6 million square miles across North Africa, the Sahara is the largest hot desert on Earth, and its mysteries have captured the imagination of explorers, writers, and adventurers for centuries. Here, amid the seemingly desolate terrain, lie secrets waiting to be uncovered.

One of the most iconic features of the Sahara is its towering sand dunes. These colossal formations, some reaching heights of over 500 feet, create a surreal and ever-changing landscape. The dunes, sculpted by the relentless winds, shift and reshape themselves, leaving behind a mesmerizing record of their movements.

The Sahara is not devoid of life, as one might assume. Surprisingly, this seemingly inhospitable desert is home to a remarkable array of flora and fauna adapted to extreme conditions. Desert-adapted plants like the hardy acacia and resilient date palms dot the landscape, providing sustenance for both wildlife and nomadic peoples.

The desert's fauna includes creatures such as the elusive Fennec fox, known for its large ears that help dissipate heat, and the agile sand gazelle, capable of surviving in this harsh environment. Birdlife is also surprisingly abundant, with species like the desert eagle owl and the graceful desert lark thriving in the arid expanses.

The Sahara is not just a geological and ecological wonder; it's a repository of history and human culture. The desert has witnessed the rise and fall of ancient civilizations, from the Carthaginians and Romans to the indigenous Berber peoples. Ruins of fortresses, trading posts, and settlements still stand as silent witnesses to the passage of time.

The Sahara's Bedouin and Tuareg nomads have traversed its vastness for centuries, following age-old trade routes and relying on their intimate knowledge of the desert's rhythms. These nomadic peoples have developed unique traditions, including intricate jewelry, vibrant textiles, and captivating music that reflect their connection to this unforgiving yet mesmerizing environment.

The Sahara's night skies are a canvas of wonder. With minimal light pollution and crisp, clear air, stargazing in the desert is a revelation. The Milky Way stretches across the heavens, and constellations that have guided travelers for generations shimmer in the darkness.

But perhaps the greatest mystery of the Sahara lies beneath its sands. Archaeological discoveries in recent years have revealed ancient rock art, hidden oases, and even buried cities that challenge our understanding of the desert's history. These findings hint at a rich tapestry of human existence in this seemingly inhospitable realm.

The Sahara's shifting sands, vast solitude, and stark beauty evoke a sense of both wonder and humility. It is a place where time and space expand, where the line between reality and imagination blurs. The mysteries of the Sahara Desert are as boundless as its dunes, inviting adventurers to explore its secrets and uncover the stories it holds, waiting to be whispered on the winds of time.

Atlas Mountains - A Trekker's Paradise

Stretching across Morocco, Algeria, and Tunisia, the Atlas Mountains form a majestic and formidable range that captivates the hearts of trekkers and adventurers from around the world. This rugged and awe-inspiring landscape offers a paradise for those who seek the thrill of exploration, the serenity of high-altitude solitude, and the breathtaking beauty of nature at its most dramatic.

The Atlas Mountains are divided into three main ranges: the High Atlas, the Middle Atlas, and the Anti-Atlas. Each range has its own unique character, offering a diverse range of trekking experiences.

The High Atlas, with its soaring peaks and deep valleys, is the most famous of the three. The tallest peak in North Africa, Mount Toubkal, rises to an impressive 13,671 feet (4,167 meters) above sea level. Summiting Mount Toubkal is a dream for many trekkers, and the reward is an unparalleled panoramic view of the surrounding mountains and valleys.

Trekking in the High Atlas takes you through remote Berber villages, where you can experience the warm hospitality of the local people. The traditional mud-brick homes, terraced fields, and centuries-old irrigation systems are a testament to the resilience of mountain communities.

The Middle Atlas, located to the north, is characterized by rolling hills, dense cedar forests, and numerous lakes. This region offers a different trekking experience, with opportunities for wildlife spotting, including Barbary macaques and a variety of bird species.

The Anti-Atlas, to the south, boasts unique geological formations, including deep canyons and striking rock formations. Trekking in this area allows you to explore the desert-like landscapes and visit hidden oasis villages where date palms thrive.

Trekking in the Atlas Mountains is not just about conquering peaks; it's about immersing yourself in a world of natural beauty and cultural richness. Along the trails, you'll encounter nomadic shepherds tending to their flocks, women crafting vibrant textiles, and the aromatic scent of traditional Moroccan cuisine wafting from rustic kitchens.

The Berber culture, deeply rooted in the Atlas Mountains, adds a rich layer to your trekking experience. Berber hospitality knows no bounds, and sharing a cup of mint tea with a local family in a remote village is a memorable part of the journey.

The changing seasons bring a kaleidoscope of colors to the Atlas Mountains. In spring, the valleys burst with wildflowers, while in autumn, the mountainsides are painted in shades of red and gold. Winter brings a blanket of snow, transforming the landscape into a winter wonderland, perfect for snowshoeing and winter trekking.

Trekking routes in the Atlas Mountains vary in difficulty, making it accessible to both novice and experienced hikers. Whether you're embarking on a multi-day expedition or a day hike, the Atlas Mountains offer a trekking paradise for all levels of outdoor enthusiasts.

As you traverse the rugged terrain, you'll be rewarded with jaw-dropping vistas of snow-capped peaks, serene mountain lakes, and terraced valleys carved into the landscape. The Atlas Mountains are a place where you can escape the demands of modern life, reconnect with nature, and savor the sense of achievement that comes from conquering their challenging trails.

In the Atlas Mountains, adventure and tranquility coexist harmoniously, offering trekkers a paradise of unparalleled natural beauty, cultural immersion, and unforgettable experiences.

Moroccan Architecture: A Blend of Traditions

Moroccan architecture stands as a testament to the rich and diverse history of this North African nation. Rooted in ancient traditions and influenced by a myriad of cultures that have left their mark on the region over the centuries, Moroccan architecture is a captivating blend of form, function, and cultural expression.

At the heart of Moroccan architecture is the concept of "riads." Riads are traditional Moroccan houses built around a central courtyard. They are characterized by their inward-facing design, with the exterior often displaying a modest facade that conceals the architectural marvels within. Riads serve both practical and cultural purposes, offering privacy and protection from the elements while creating an oasis of tranquility and beauty.

One of the most distinctive features of Moroccan architecture is the use of geometric patterns and intricate tilework. Zellige, a form of mosaic tilework, adorns walls, floors, and ceilings with colorful and mesmerizing patterns. The intricate artistry of zellige is a hallmark of Moroccan design, and it is seen in palaces, mosques, and homes alike.

The Alhambra Palace in Spain is a testament to the enduring influence of Moroccan architecture. The intricate stucco work, horseshoe arches, and geometric tile patterns found in the Alhambra bear striking resemblance to Moroccan architectural elements. This is no coincidence, as the Moors who once ruled Spain were themselves influenced by Moroccan design.

Moroccan architecture also reflects the nation's Islamic heritage. Mosques, with their minarets and prayer halls adorned with calligraphy and geometric patterns, are not only places of worship but also architectural marvels. The Koutoubia Mosque in Marrakech, with its towering minaret and beautiful gardens, is a prime example of Moroccan Islamic architecture.

The kasbahs of Morocco are another architectural wonder. These fortress-like structures are made of earthen materials, blending seamlessly with the surrounding landscape. The Kasbah of Ait Ben Haddou, a UNESCO World Heritage Site, is a prime example of this ancient architectural style. Kasbahs served as both protective fortifications and hubs of trade and culture along historic caravan routes.

Moroccan architecture is also marked by its use of natural materials. The warm hues of earthen clay, stone, and wood are not only visually pleasing but also help regulate temperature, keeping interiors cool in the scorching desert heat. The use of natural materials is not just practical but also a nod to sustainability, a concept that has been ingrained in Moroccan architecture for centuries.

Traditional Moroccan houses often feature intricately carved wooden doors and windows, adding to the overall aesthetic. These wooden elements are not only decorative but also serve as functional features, allowing for natural ventilation while providing privacy.

In recent years, contemporary Moroccan architecture has evolved to blend modern design with traditional elements.

Architects and designers have embraced the challenge of preserving Morocco's architectural heritage while creating spaces that cater to modern lifestyles and needs.

Moroccan architecture is not confined to a single style but rather a dynamic fusion of influences, traditions, and creativity. It is a reflection of Morocco's rich history, diverse cultural heritage, and the enduring commitment to craftsmanship and artistry. As you explore the streets of Moroccan cities or venture into remote villages, you'll find that Moroccan architecture is not just about buildings; it's about storytelling, cultural preservation, and the enduring beauty of a nation's creative spirit.

The Souks of Morocco: A Shopper's Delight

When you step into the bustling souks of Morocco, you enter a world where shopping is not just a transaction; it's an immersive cultural experience that has been perfected over centuries. The souks, vibrant marketplaces found in Moroccan cities, are a shopper's delight, offering an array of goods that tantalize the senses and beckon you to explore their winding alleys and hidden treasures.

Marrakech, with its famous Jemaa el-Fnaa square, is a sensory overload of sights, sounds, and scents. As you weave your way through the labyrinthine medina, you'll encounter vendors selling everything from colorful textiles and handcrafted jewelry to aromatic spices and traditional pottery. The souks of Marrakech are a kaleidoscope of colors, with vibrant textiles and intricately patterned carpets on display at every turn.

Fez, Morocco's ancient cultural and intellectual capital, boasts one of the most renowned souks in the country. The Medina of Fez is a UNESCO World Heritage Site, and its souks are a testament to the city's artisanal traditions. The leather tanneries of Fez, where hides are dyed using age-old techniques, are a must-visit. You can watch as workers laboriously craft leather goods such as bags, shoes, and jackets, all available for purchase.

The city of Chefchaouen, known for its blue-painted streets, is home to a unique souk experience. Here, you'll find an array of handicrafts and textiles in shades of blue, echoing the town's distinctive aesthetic. Shopping in Chefchaouen's souks feels like uncovering hidden treasures in a serene mountain setting.

Essaouira's souks, set against a backdrop of crashing waves and sea breezes, offer a more relaxed shopping experience. The town is famous for its woodworking artisans, and you can browse stalls selling finely crafted wooden furniture, instruments, and art. The medina is also home to a thriving art scene, with galleries showcasing the works of local and international artists.

In the souks, haggling is not just accepted; it's expected. Bargaining is a time-honored tradition, and skilled shoppers can often secure excellent deals. However, it's essential to approach haggling with respect and good humor, as it's considered a friendly exchange rather than a confrontation.

Morocco's souks are not just about shopping; they're about cultural exchange. As you engage with vendors, you'll discover stories behind the products, learn about traditional craftsmanship, and gain insight into the daily lives of the people who call these markets home. Sharing a cup of mint tea during a negotiation is a common practice, fostering connections and conversations that transcend commerce.

Food enthusiasts will find the souks equally enticing. Moroccan cuisine is celebrated for its rich flavors and aromatic spices, and the souks are where you can stock up on ingredients such as saffron, cumin, and preserved lemons. You can also indulge in street food delights like savory pastries, grilled meats, and freshly squeezed fruit juices.

The souks are not limited to physical goods. Traditional Moroccan music, performed by local musicians, adds to the lively atmosphere. You may encounter snake charmers, storytellers, and artisans practicing their craft right before your eyes.

While the souks are a treasure trove of goods, they are also an embodiment of Morocco's cultural diversity. Berber, Arab, and African influences converge in these marketplaces, showcasing the nation's rich heritage. The souks are a place where tradition and modernity intersect, where centuries-old craftsmanship meets contemporary design.

Exploring the souks of Morocco is an adventure in itself, a journey that engages all your senses and introduces you to the heart and soul of the country. Each alleyway, each stall, and each interaction tells a story, inviting you to be a part of Morocco's vibrant tapestry of commerce, culture, and community.

Moroccan Arts and Crafts

Moroccan arts and crafts are a testament to the country's rich cultural heritage and the enduring craftsmanship of its people. Rooted in centuries-old traditions and influenced by a blend of Berber, Arab, and African cultures, Moroccan artisans create an exquisite tapestry of handmade goods that span a wide spectrum of artistic disciplines.

Textiles are an integral part of Moroccan craftsmanship, and the country is renowned for its vibrant and intricate fabrics. The ancient art of weaving produces a stunning array of textiles, from sumptuous carpets with geometric patterns to finely embroidered garments. The city of Fes, in particular, is known for its intricate silk brocades and velvet textiles.

One of Morocco's most iconic textile creations is the Berber rug. These handwoven rugs are often characterized by bold geometric designs and vibrant colors. Each rug tells a unique story, reflecting the weaver's creativity and the region's traditions. The process of creating a Berber rug is labor-intensive, with artisans using natural dyes and traditional techniques passed down through generations.

Pottery and ceramics hold a special place in Moroccan arts and crafts. The city of Safi is famous for its blue and white pottery, adorned with intricate patterns and designs. The vibrant blue hues are reminiscent of the sea and sky, and these ceramics are both decorative and functional, with traditional tea sets and tagine dishes being popular items.

Metalwork is another celebrated craft in Morocco. Skilled artisans create intricate lamps, lanterns, and decorative pieces from brass, copper, and silver. The city of Marrakech is known for its elaborate metalwork, often featuring filigree patterns that cast mesmerizing patterns of light and shadow when illuminated.

Woodworking is a cherished tradition in Moroccan craftsmanship. From ornate doors and windows to finely carved furniture and intricate lattice screens known as "moucharabieh," woodwork in Morocco showcases meticulous craftsmanship. The scent of cedar, a commonly used wood, fills the air in many Moroccan homes.

The art of leatherwork is exemplified in the souks of Marrakech and Fez. Skilled tanners use traditional methods to dye and treat animal hides, creating leather goods such as bags, shoes, and poufs. The tanneries in Fez are particularly famous, and you can witness the fascinating process of dyeing leather in large vats filled with natural pigments.

Morocco's jewelry is a fusion of ancient traditions and contemporary design. The souks offer a dazzling array of jewelry, from intricate silver Berber pieces to contemporary designs that incorporate semi-precious stones and traditional motifs. Many pieces are handmade by skilled artisans, making each jewelry item a work of art.

Intricate calligraphy and illuminated manuscripts are also part of Morocco's artistic heritage. Arabic calligraphy, with its flowing and elegant script, often adorns architectural elements, manuscripts, and artwork. The blending of calligraphy with geometric patterns and floral motifs is a hallmark of Moroccan design.

Moroccan arts and crafts are deeply intertwined with the country's cultural and religious traditions. Many artisans draw inspiration from Islamic architecture and design, incorporating elements such as arabesques, geometric shapes, and intricate tilework into their creations.

The creation of Moroccan arts and crafts is not just a livelihood; it's a labor of love that preserves centuries-old traditions. Many artisans belong to craft cooperatives and families with a long history of craftsmanship. These cooperatives ensure fair wages, the sustainability of traditional techniques, and the continuation of cultural heritage.

Exploring Moroccan arts and crafts is not merely a shopping experience; it's a journey through the country's history, culture, and creativity. Each piece tells a story of Morocco's past and present, offering a tangible connection to the artisans who pour their skill and passion into their craft.

Music and Dance: The Rhythms of Morocco

In Morocco, the beating heart of culture is found in its music and dance. It's a world where the rhythms of the past merge seamlessly with the energy of the present, creating a vibrant tapestry of sound and movement that reflects the nation's diverse heritage and enduring creativity.

Moroccan music is a mosaic of influences, and it begins with the indigenous Berber traditions that have thrived in North Africa for millennia. The Amazigh people, as the Berbers are known locally, have their unique styles of music that incorporate the use of traditional instruments like the "ribab" (a single-stringed fiddle) and the "tam-tam" (a type of drum). Berber music often conveys stories of daily life, history, and the natural world.

With the arrival of Islam came the integration of Arabic music into Moroccan culture. Arabic music, with its distinctive scales and vocal styles, became an integral part of Morocco's musical landscape. The "oud," a pear-shaped string instrument, and the "qanun," a zither-like instrument, are central to Arabic music and have made their mark on Moroccan compositions.

Morocco's geographic location, at the crossroads of Africa, Europe, and the Middle East, has also infused its music with international flavors. The Gnaoua music of Morocco, for example, is deeply influenced by sub-Saharan African rhythms and melodies. It's characterized by the use of the "guembri" (a three-stringed bass instrument) and hypnotic percussion. Gnaoua music is often associated with trance-like rituals and is celebrated during the annual Gnaoua World Music Festival in Essaouira.

The Andalusian influence, hailing from Spain, is another significant aspect of Moroccan music. Andalusian music is characterized by intricate melodies, virtuoso instrumental performances, and poetic lyrics. The "nay" (a reed flute) and "darbuka" (a goblet drum) feature prominently in Andalusian orchestras. The city of Fes is particularly known for its Andalusian music traditions.

Moroccan music is not confined to the concert stage; it's woven into the fabric of daily life. You'll hear street musicians playing traditional tunes in medina squares, impromptu gatherings of friends and family breaking into song, and the lively sounds of percussion instruments accompanying celebratory events like weddings and festivals.

Moroccan dance is inseparable from the music that accompanies it. The nation boasts a diverse range of dance styles, each with its unique movements and significance. The "Ahidous," a Berber group dance, is a powerful expression of unity and community, often performed at weddings and festive occasions. The "Chaabi" dance, characterized by lively footwork and graceful arm movements, is a staple of Moroccan folk dance.

The mesmerizing "Guedra" dance of the Tuareg people in the Sahara Desert is a symbolic ritual performed by women. It involves intricate hand movements, rhythmic chanting, and the wearing of veils, creating an otherworldly atmosphere that reflects the mystique of the desert.

And then there's the "Belly Dance," known as "Raqs Sharqi" in Arabic, which has its variations in Morocco. This dance, characterized by undulating movements of the torso and hips, has captivated audiences worldwide. It's often performed at restaurants and special events, adding a touch of exoticism to the atmosphere.

Moroccan music and dance are not static; they continue to evolve. Contemporary Moroccan artists blend traditional elements with modern genres, creating a dynamic fusion of sounds. Hip-hop, rap, and electronic music have found a place in Morocco's music scene, providing a platform for self-expression and social commentary.

The cultural significance of music and dance in Morocco cannot be overstated. They serve as a medium for storytelling, preserving history and traditions, and fostering a sense of identity and belonging. Whether you're tapping your foot to the rhythms of a street performer or experiencing the energy of a traditional dance troupe, Morocco's music and dance are a testament to the power of art to connect people across time and borders.

Festivals and Celebrations Across the Year

Morocco is a land of celebrations, where traditions and festivities paint the calendar with vibrant colors, lively music, and joyous gatherings throughout the year. These festivals are a testament to the country's rich cultural diversity, its deep-rooted traditions, and the spirit of unity that defines its people.

One of the most prominent festivals in Morocco is Eid al-Fitr, which marks the end of Ramadan, the holy month of fasting for Muslims. Families come together to break their fast with special meals, and it's a time for giving and receiving gifts, especially for children. The streets come alive with colorful decorations, and mosques are filled with worshippers attending special prayers.

Another significant Islamic festival is Eid al-Adha, known as the "Festival of Sacrifice." It commemorates the willingness of Abraham (Ibrahim in Islamic tradition) to sacrifice his son as an act of obedience to God. Families gather to sacrifice an animal, typically a sheep or goat, and share the meat with relatives and those in need. It's a time of giving and charity.

Morocco's cultural tapestry extends to the Jewish community, who celebrate the holiday of Purim with great enthusiasm. The town of Essaouira is known for its unique Jewish Purim celebrations, where locals and tourists alike join in the festivities, wearing costumes, sharing traditional pastries called "hamantaschen," and enjoying parades and music.

Gnaoua World Music Festival in Essaouira is a world-renowned event that celebrates the fusion of music and spirituality. It's a four-day extravaganza where Gnaoua musicians from Morocco and around the world come together to perform hypnotic music, characterized by rhythmic chants and percussion. The festival showcases the country's rich musical heritage.

The Rose Festival in the town of Kelaat M'Gouna is a fragrant celebration of the Damask rose harvest. The air is filled with the sweet scent of roses, and locals create intricate designs with rose petals. The festival features music, dance, and a colorful parade that winds through the town's rose-covered streets.

Imilchil Marriage Festival, held in the Atlas Mountains, is a unique cultural event where local Berber tribes gather to celebrate love and marriage. The festival is an opportunity for young people to meet potential partners and for families to negotiate marriages. It's a time of song, dance, and matchmaking amidst stunning mountain landscapes.

The International Film Festival of Marrakech is a significant event in the country's cultural calendar. It attracts filmmakers, actors, and cinema enthusiasts from around the world. The festival showcases a diverse range of films and serves as a platform for emerging talent.

Morocco also celebrates its Independence Day on March 2nd, commemorating the country's independence from French and Spanish colonial rule in 1956. Parades, concerts, and patriotic displays mark this national holiday, reflecting the pride Moroccans have in their sovereignty.

Mawazine Festival in Rabat is one of the largest music festivals in Africa, featuring international and Moroccan artists across various genres. It's a week-long celebration of music and culture, drawing crowds of music enthusiasts from all over the world.

These festivals and celebrations in Morocco are more than just events on the calendar; they are a reflection of the nation's soul and its enduring commitment to preserving traditions while embracing diversity. They offer a glimpse into the warmth, hospitality, and exuberance of the Moroccan people, inviting visitors to share in the joy of these vibrant cultural expressions throughout the year.

Moroccan Hospitality: Riads and Guesthouses

In Morocco, hospitality is not merely a custom; it's a way of life deeply ingrained in the culture and ethos of the people. Travelers to this North African gem often find themselves enveloped in a warm embrace of Moroccan hospitality, and a significant aspect of this experience is the accommodation known as riads and guesthouses.

A riad, pronounced "ree-ad," is a traditional Moroccan house or palace with an inward-facing design, typically organized around a central courtyard or garden. The word "riad" itself is derived from the Arabic term for garden. These architectural gems serve as a haven of tranquility and comfort amid the bustling streets of Morocco's cities.

Riads are often hidden behind unassuming entrances in the narrow alleyways of ancient medinas, making them delightful surprises for travelers. The exterior walls are plain and modest, offering little indication of the enchantment that lies within. Once inside, you'll discover a world of elegance, beauty, and cultural richness.

The central courtyard of a riad is a focal point, adorned with intricate tilework, lush plants, and often a refreshing fountain. This space is not only aesthetically pleasing but also serves as a gathering area where guests can relax, enjoy meals, or simply soak in the serene atmosphere.

Many riads are family-run establishments, and the personal touch is evident in every detail. The owners and staff take pride in ensuring that guests feel like an extension of their family, providing attentive service and warm hospitality. It's not uncommon for guests to be welcomed with a refreshing glass of Moroccan mint tea upon arrival.

The architecture of riads is a harmonious blend of Moroccan and Islamic design elements. Arched doorways, intricate plasterwork, and ornate woodcarvings adorn the interiors. Zellige, the colorful mosaic tilework, often graces the walls and floors, creating a mesmerizing visual experience.

Guest rooms in riads are thoughtfully designed, offering a blend of comfort and authenticity. Many rooms feature traditional Moroccan furnishings, including carved wooden beds, rich textiles, and local artwork. Modern amenities are seamlessly integrated, providing guests with all the comforts they need while preserving the riad's traditional charm.

Meals in riads are a culinary journey through Moroccan cuisine. Traditional Moroccan dishes like tagine, couscous, and pastries are often served, showcasing the country's rich and flavorful gastronomy. Many riads offer the option of dining on a rooftop terrace with panoramic views of the city and surrounding landscapes.

Moroccan guesthouses, known as "dar" (meaning "house" in Arabic), offer a similar hospitality experience. These smaller-scale accommodations provide an intimate setting for travelers seeking a deeper connection with Moroccan culture. Dars are often tucked away in historic neighborhoods, offering an authentic and immersive stay.

Staying in a riad or dar provides more than just lodging; it's an opportunity to connect with the local community and gain insights into Moroccan traditions and way of life. Owners and staff are often happy to share stories, recommend local experiences, and arrange activities to enhance your visit.

Whether you choose a riad or dar, the experience is a journey into the heart of Moroccan hospitality. It's a chance to immerse yourself in the country's rich cultural heritage while enjoying the comforts and elegance of these unique accommodations. As you step out of the bustling medina into the tranquil oasis of a riad or dar, you'll find that Moroccan hospitality is not just a gesture; it's a heartfelt expression of warmth and welcome that leaves a lasting impression on every traveler.

Moroccan Dress and Traditional Attire

The attire of Morocco is a vibrant tapestry woven with history, culture, and identity. It reflects the diverse influences that have shaped the country's fashion over the centuries, from indigenous Berber traditions to the intricate designs of Islamic and Andalusian influence. Moroccan dress is a fascinating fusion of old and new, showcasing a blend of traditional garments and modern styles.

One of the most iconic pieces of Moroccan clothing is the "djellaba." This long, loose-fitting robe is typically made from cotton or wool and is a staple in the wardrobes of both men and women. The djellaba is not only comfortable but also functional, providing protection from the elements, especially in Morocco's varying climates.

The "caftan" is another renowned Moroccan garment, known for its elegance and versatility. Originally influenced by Persian fashion, the caftan has evolved into a symbol of Moroccan high fashion. Caftans are often richly decorated with intricate embroidery, beading, and embellishments, making them a popular choice for special occasions, weddings, and celebrations.

Turban-like head coverings known as "shesh" or "chechia" are commonly worn by Moroccan men. These headpieces are not only stylish but also provide protection from the sun and heat. The colors and styles of the shesh can vary by region, and they are often coordinated with the rest of the outfit.

Traditional Berber clothing varies among the different Berber tribes, each with its unique style and patterns. The "haik" is a common garment among Berber women, consisting of a large piece of fabric that is draped elegantly around the body and often worn with a belt. Berber men may wear the "takchita," a traditional outfit comprising a robe and a hood.

In rural areas, it's common to see men and women wearing "jabadors," which are simpler, less embellished versions of the djellaba. These practical garments are well-suited for the demands of agricultural and outdoor work.

The "kaftan" is a variation of the caftan, primarily worn by men. It's characterized by its straight-line cut and minimalistic design. Kaftans are often worn for formal occasions and are sometimes paired with a "tarbouch," a fez-like hat.

Moroccan women are known for their intricate and artistic henna tattoos, often applied to their hands and feet during special occasions and celebrations. These temporary tattoos are not only a form of adornment but also a cultural expression.

In urban areas, especially among the younger generation, Western-style clothing is prevalent. Jeans, t-shirts, and modern dresses are commonly worn in Moroccan cities, reflecting the influence of globalization and contemporary fashion trends.

It's important to note that Morocco's dress code can vary significantly between urban and rural areas, as well as by region and occasion. While urban areas tend to be more relaxed in terms of attire, rural and conservative regions may adhere to more traditional dress codes.

Moroccan attire is not just about clothing; it's a visual language that communicates aspects of identity, culture, and occasion. The choice of garments often reflects a balance between tradition and modernity, allowing Moroccans to express their heritage while embracing contemporary styles. Whether it's the timeless elegance of a caftan, the practicality of a djellaba, or the fusion of global fashion, Moroccan dress tells a story that continues to evolve in a changing world.

Moroccan Henna Art and Tattoos

Morocco is a land of artistry, and one of its most captivating and cherished artistic expressions is henna art. The tradition of adorning the body with henna, known as "mehndi" in Morocco, is a cultural practice that has endured for centuries. This intricate form of body art is more than just a decorative element; it's a visual language that communicates beauty, symbolism, and tradition.

Henna, scientifically known as "Lawsonia inermis," is a plant that grows abundantly in Morocco. Its leaves are harvested, dried, and crushed into a fine powder, which is then mixed with water to create a paste. This paste is what's used to create the exquisite designs on the skin.

Moroccan henna art is characterized by its elaborate and detailed patterns, often inspired by geometric shapes, nature, and traditional motifs. These designs are not merely random or ornamental; they carry deep cultural significance. Each element, each line, and each curve has a story to tell.

Henna art in Morocco is an integral part of celebrations and special occasions. It's not uncommon to see Moroccan women and sometimes men, too, with henna designs on their hands and feet during weddings, festivals, and other momentous events. These designs are a form of adornment, a celebration of beauty, and a reflection of the joyous spirit of the occasion.

Weddings, in particular, are a significant canvas for henna art. Moroccan brides often undergo a special pre-wedding henna ceremony, known as "Henna Night" or "Laylat al-Henna." During this ceremony, the bride's hands and feet are intricately adorned with henna designs that can take hours to complete. It's a bonding moment with family and friends, and the designs are believed to bring blessings, protection, and good fortune to the newlyweds.

In addition to weddings, henna is also a part of religious celebrations, such as Eid al-Fitr and Eid al-Adha. Many Moroccans decorate their hands with henna during these holidays as a way of enhancing their appearance and celebrating the festive atmosphere.

Henna art is not confined to celebratory occasions; it's a year-round form of self-expression. Women and sometimes men visit local henna artists or apply henna themselves to mark special moments, express their creativity, or simply enhance their appearance. The beauty of henna is that it's temporary, allowing individuals to change their designs regularly.

Henna artists in Morocco are skilled artisans who have mastered the art of creating intricate and symmetrical patterns. Their expertise is often passed down through generations, with techniques and designs being shared within families and communities.

The process of applying henna involves careful precision. The artist uses a fine-tipped applicator or a cone to create the intricate designs. After the henna paste is applied, it needs time to dry and set. Once it's removed, the skin beneath is stained with a reddish-brown hue that darkens over the following days. The final color and duration of the stain can vary depending on factors like the quality of henna, the design complexity, and individual skin characteristics.

Henna art is more than just a form of body decoration; it's a reflection of Morocco's rich cultural heritage, a celebration of life's milestones, and a connection to the traditions of the past. Whether it's adorning a bride on her wedding day or simply embracing the beauty of intricate designs, henna art is a living testament to the enduring creativity and artistic spirit of Morocco.

Moroccan Weddings and Ceremonies

Moroccan weddings and ceremonies are a vibrant tapestry of tradition, celebration, and cultural richness. These events are not merely gatherings; they are grand affairs that reflect the deep-rooted customs and values of Moroccan society. A Moroccan wedding is a journey through time and tradition, a joyful union of families, and a showcase of the country's diverse cultural heritage.

Moroccan weddings are known for their elaborate and multifaceted celebrations, which can span several days. They begin with pre-wedding rituals and culminate in a grand wedding ceremony. The entire process is a meticulous and joyful affair, marked by intricate customs and timeless traditions.

One of the most iconic pre-wedding rituals is the "Henna Night" or "Laylat al-Henna." This is a special evening dedicated to adorning the bride with intricate henna designs on her hands and feet. Family members and friends gather to celebrate and take part in this ancient tradition. The designs, often elaborate and detailed, are believed to bring blessings, good fortune, and protection to the bride.

The "Hammam" or traditional Moroccan bath is another essential pre-wedding ritual. The bride and groom, separately, undergo a cleansing and beautification process that includes exfoliation, massages, and skin treatments. It's a time for relaxation and preparation, ensuring that they look their best on the big day.

Moroccan weddings are known for their opulent attire. Brides often wear elaborate caftans, intricately embroidered and adorned with jewelry, while grooms opt for stylish and equally ornate traditional attire. The colors and designs of the wedding outfits are carefully selected, often symbolizing aspects of the couple's journey and their families.

The wedding ceremony itself is a grand affair, often held in a lavish venue or the bride's family home. Moroccan weddings are known for their festive and joyful atmosphere. Music, dance, and traditional Moroccan instruments, like the "oud" and "tabla," create a lively and captivating ambiance.

A key moment in the ceremony is the "Amariya" or "Takharbat," where the bride is led to the groom's side by her female relatives, symbolizing her transition from her family to her new life with her husband. This moment is filled with emotion and tradition.

The "Achoura" is a customary game played at Moroccan weddings, symbolizing the couple's journey through life together. It involves a bowl of milk and various objects, each representing a different aspect of life. The bride and groom must find the objects without using their hands, emphasizing teamwork and cooperation.

Moroccan weddings are also renowned for their culinary delights. Traditional dishes like tagine, couscous, pastries, and Moroccan sweets are served in abundance. It's a feast for the senses, with flavors and aromas that reflect Morocco's rich culinary heritage.

The "Zaffa" or wedding procession is a highlight of Moroccan weddings. It's a lively and colorful parade that includes traditional music, dancers, and the bride and groom being carried on ornate thrones. The Zaffa moves through the streets, inviting the community to join in the celebration.

Moroccan weddings are not just about the couple; they are community events that bring families, friends, and neighbors together. They are an opportunity to strengthen bonds, share joy, and honor age-old traditions.

These weddings and ceremonies are a testament to Morocco's cultural diversity and the importance of preserving traditions in a changing world. They are a celebration of love, family, and heritage, and they offer a glimpse into the rich tapestry of Moroccan life and customs.

The Moroccan Language: Arabic and Amazigh

Language is the heartbeat of culture, and in Morocco, it beats with a fascinating blend of Arabic and Amazigh, creating a linguistic mosaic that reflects the nation's rich and diverse heritage. These two languages, intertwined with history and culture, serve as the vibrant threads that weave Morocco's linguistic tapestry.

Arabic is the official language of Morocco, and Moroccan Arabic, also known as "Darija," is the predominant dialect spoken by the majority of Moroccans. While Darija shares many linguistic elements with Standard Arabic, it has evolved over the centuries to include significant influences from Amazigh, French, Spanish, and other languages. As a result, Moroccan Arabic is uniquely Moroccan, rich in regional variations, idioms, and expressions.

Darija serves as the language of everyday communication, used in homes, markets, streets, and social gatherings. It is a testament to Morocco's cultural diversity, with regional accents and dialects reflecting the nuances of different areas across the country. While many Moroccans are fluent in Darija, it may present challenges for foreign speakers due to its colloquial nature and variations.

In addition to Darija, Standard Arabic, also known as "Al-Fusha," is taught in schools and used in formal contexts. It is the language of education, media, government, and religion. Learning Standard Arabic is a fundamental part of the Moroccan education system, ensuring that Moroccans have access to their country's literary and religious heritage.

Amazigh, also known as "Tamazight," is another integral component of Morocco's linguistic landscape. It is the language of the Amazigh people, who are indigenous to North Africa and have a deep historical presence in Morocco. Tamazight is a family of closely related languages and dialects, with regional variations across Morocco's Amazigh communities.

Efforts to promote and preserve the Amazigh language have gained momentum in recent years, with Tamazight being recognized as an official language alongside Arabic in the Moroccan constitution. Schools now offer Tamazight language classes, and there are ongoing initiatives to revitalize and standardize the language, ensuring its continued presence in Moroccan society.

French is also widely spoken and holds an important place in Morocco's linguistic landscape. It is often used in business, administration, and education, particularly in higher education. The legacy of French colonialism has left a lasting influence on Moroccan society, making French proficiency an asset in various professional fields.

Spanish, especially in northern regions of Morocco, is prevalent due to the country's proximity to Spain. Spanish influence is evident in the culture, architecture, and even the local cuisine of these areas.

English, while not as widespread as French and Spanish, is gaining popularity, particularly among the younger generation. It is seen as a valuable skill for global communication and opportunities in tourism and international business.

Morocco's linguistic diversity is not only a reflection of its historical interactions with different cultures and peoples but also a source of strength and resilience. The ability to speak multiple languages is highly regarded in Moroccan society, and many Moroccans are proficient in several languages, enabling them to engage with a globalized world while maintaining their unique cultural identity.

In this linguistic tapestry, Arabic and Amazigh remain at the core of Morocco's identity, connecting the past with the present and shaping the nation's future. Together, they serve as a testament to the enduring spirit of Morocco, where language is not just a means of communication but a celebration of cultural diversity and heritage.

Dialects and the Role of French

Morocco's linguistic landscape is a tapestry of dialects, each adding a unique thread to the rich fabric of the country's language. While Arabic and Amazigh form the foundation of communication, dialects play a crucial role in shaping the nuances of everyday conversations and cultural expressions.

Dialects are regional or community-specific variations of a language, often characterized by distinctive vocabulary, pronunciation, and grammar. In Morocco, Darija, or Moroccan Arabic, serves as the primary language of daily life, but it comes in various regional flavors, each influenced by historical and cultural factors.

One of the most notable dialects is "Casablanca Darija," spoken in Morocco's economic hub, Casablanca. This dialect carries a reputation for its modern and cosmopolitan influences due to the city's international connections. It incorporates French loanwords and expressions, reflecting the city's historical ties to French colonialism and its role as a business and cultural center.

In the capital city, Rabat, a slightly different dialect is spoken, known as "Rabati Darija." While it shares similarities with Casablanca Darija, it has its unique local expressions and vocabulary. This reflects the distinctive identity of the capital and its residents.

The northern regions of Morocco, particularly those close to Spain, have dialects that incorporate Spanish words and phrases. The historical proximity and interactions with

Spanish-speaking regions have left a linguistic imprint on these areas. For example, in Tetouan, you might hear a blend of Spanish and Moroccan Arabic, showcasing the multicultural heritage of the region.

In the southern parts of Morocco, such as Marrakech, "Marrakechi Darija" has its own distinct character. With a blend of Berber influences, it reflects the city's vibrant cultural heritage. Traveling across Morocco, you'll encounter many other regional dialects, each with its unique charm and flavor.

Now, let's talk about the role of French in Morocco's linguistic landscape. French, a legacy of colonial rule, has maintained a prominent position in Moroccan society. It is often used in formal settings, including education, business, and government. Many Moroccans are bilingual in French and Arabic, and proficiency in French is considered an asset in various professional fields.

French influence is particularly evident in urban areas and among the educated elite. Street signs, official documents, and higher education often use French alongside Arabic. This bilingualism facilitates communication with French-speaking countries and opens doors to international opportunities.

In schools, Moroccan students are typically taught in Arabic, with French as a second language. This bilingual education system has created a generation of Moroccans who are comfortable navigating both linguistic worlds.

In recent years, there has been a growing interest in English, especially among the younger generation. English is seen as a global language of communication, and proficiency in English is sought after in fields like tourism, technology, and international business.

Despite the prominence of French and the growing interest in English, Moroccan Arabic remains the language of the heart, the language of daily life, and the language that connects Moroccans from different regions and backgrounds. Dialects add the spice of regional identity, enriching the linguistic landscape with their unique flavors.

In this dynamic linguistic mosaic, Morocco continues to evolve, embracing its multicultural heritage while adapting to the demands of a changing world. Language, as always, remains a reflection of identity, culture, and the intricate tapestry of Morocco's past and present.

Learning Moroccan Arabic for Travelers

Embarking on a journey to Morocco is like stepping into a world where history, culture, and traditions converge. As you traverse this enchanting country, one of the most rewarding experiences is engaging with the locals, and to truly connect, a bit of knowledge in Moroccan Arabic can go a long way.

Moroccan Arabic, known as "Darija," is the heartbeat of everyday communication in Morocco. While many Moroccans are bilingual and may speak French, Spanish, or English, speaking their native Darija shows a genuine appreciation for their culture and a desire to connect on a deeper level. Learning some basic Moroccan Arabic phrases and expressions can enhance your travel experience and open doors to meaningful interactions.

Greetings and Polite Expressions:

1. *Salam alaykum* (سلام يكم ل ع) - This is the standard Arabic greeting, meaning "peace be upon you." It's a polite way to start conversations.
2. *Labas?* (باس ل) - A common way to ask "How are you?" in Moroccan Arabic.
3. *Shukran* (شكراً) - This means "thank you" and is always appreciated.
4. *Afak* (ع فاك) - Use this polite expression when making a request, similar to "please."
5. *La, shukran* (شكراً لا،) - If you want to politely decline something, say "no, thank you."

Basic Phrases:

6. *Naam* (نعم) - "Yes"
7. *La* (لا) - "No"
8. *Kayn* (كاين) - "There is" or "there are"
9. *Bghit* (بغيت) - "I want"
10. *Ma fhemtsh* (ما فهمتش) - "I don't understand"
11. *Wash smitk?* (واش سميتك؟) - "What's your name?"
12. *Ana smiti...* (أنا سميتي...) - "My name is..."

Numbers:

13. *Wa7ed* (واحد) - "One"
14. *Juj* (جوج) - "Two"
15. *Tlata* (تلاتة) - "Three"
16. *Arba* (أربعة) - "Four"
17. *Khamsa* (خمسة) - "Five"
18. *Sitta* (ستة) - "Six"
19. *Saba* (سبعة) - "Seven"
20. *Tmana* (ثمانية) - "Eight"
21. *Tiswa* (تسعة) - "Nine"
22. *3ashra* (عشرة) - "Ten"

Navigational Phrases:

23. *Wayn...?* (وين...) - "Where is...?"
24. *Bghit...* (بغيت...) - "I want..."
25. *Kam kayen?* (كم كاين؟) - "How much does it cost?"
26. *3afak, darori* (عفاك، داروري) - "Excuse me, I'm lost."

Food and Dining:

27. *Shay* (شاي) - "Tea," a Moroccan staple.
28. *Tbiba* (طبيبة) - "Delicious"

29. *La'chla* (لأ شلا) - "Spicy"
30. *L'ftur* (الـ فطور) - "Breakfast"
31. *L'ghada* (الـ غداء) - "Lunch"
32. *L3asha* (الـ عـ شاء) - "Dinner"

Shopping:

33. *Bi sh7al hada?* (هلدا؟ بـ شحال) - "How much is this?"
34. *Bghit hada* (هلدا بـ غـ يت) - "I want this."
35. *Ghadi nfaddlo* (نفدّلو غادي) - "I'll give you a discount."

Emergency Phrases:

36. *M'dertsh bala* (بـ لا دارتـ ش ما) - "I didn't do anything."
37. *Kan khassni hadak* (هلدك خاـ صـ ني كـان) - "I need help."
38. *Police* (بـ ولـ يس) - "Police"

While learning Moroccan Arabic can greatly enhance your travel experience, it's essential to remember that many Moroccans appreciate your efforts to speak their language, even if it's just a few words. Don't be discouraged by language barriers; a smile and a willingness to engage can bridge cultural gaps.

As you explore Morocco, you'll find that Darija is not just a mode of communication; it's a key to unlocking the warmth and hospitality of the Moroccan people. So, embrace the journey of learning and immerse yourself in the vibrant linguistic mosaic of this captivating country.

Moroccan Literature and Poetic Traditions

Morocco's literary heritage is a tapestry woven from the threads of its rich history, diverse cultures, and enduring poetic traditions. It's a land where storytelling and the written word have flourished for centuries, leaving an indelible mark on its cultural identity.

Historical Roots of Moroccan Literature:

Moroccan literature traces its origins back to the Arab invasion of North Africa in the 7th century and the subsequent spread of Islam. As Arabic became the language of religion, science, and culture, it laid the foundation for literary expression in Morocco. Early works of religious and philosophical literature emerged, including texts on jurisprudence, theology, and ethics.

The Almoravid Dynasty and Andalusian Influence:

During the reign of the Almoravid dynasty in the 11th and 12th centuries, Morocco witnessed a surge in intellectual and literary activity. The Almoravids, known for their religious zeal, promoted scholarship and the arts. They also established the University of Al-Qarawiyyin in Fez, recognized by UNESCO as the world's oldest continually operating degree-granting university.

One of the most significant literary influences during this period was the influx of Andalusian scholars and poets who sought refuge in Morocco following the fall of Muslim rule in Spain. These exiles brought with them a rich literary tradition, and their contributions greatly enriched Moroccan literature. The blending of Andalusian and Moroccan styles gave rise to a unique poetic form known as "muwashshahat."

The Berber Influence:

Morocco's indigenous Amazigh population, with its distinct languages and cultures, has also made a profound impact on the nation's literature. Amazigh poetry and oral traditions have been preserved and continue to influence contemporary Moroccan literature.

Moroccan Arabic Poetry:

Moroccan Arabic poetry, often composed in the form of "qasidas" (odes), "ghazals," and "malhun" (popular poetry), has flourished for centuries. Prominent poets like Muhammad al-Ifrani, Ahmed al-Yusufi, and Abdellatif Laabi have made significant contributions to the Moroccan literary landscape. Themes in Moroccan poetry often revolve around love, nature, spirituality, and social issues.

Novelists and Prose Writers:

In the modern era, Moroccan literature has expanded into the realm of novels and prose. Authors like Driss Chraibi, Tahar Ben Jelloun, and Leila Abouzeid have gained international recognition for their works, which explore themes of identity, tradition, and the clash between modernity and tradition.

Literature and Moroccan Identity:

Moroccan literature serves as a reflection of the country's diverse cultural heritage and complex identity. It encapsulates the dynamic interplay between Arab, Berber, Andalusian, and European influences. It's a testament to Morocco's ability to embrace its past while navigating the challenges of the present.

Oral Traditions:

In addition to written literature, Morocco boasts a vibrant tradition of oral storytelling. Storytellers known as "hlaykia" or "qussas" continue to captivate audiences with their tales of history, legends, and morality.

Morocco's literary heritage is a testament to the enduring power of words to convey the beauty, complexity, and resilience of a nation. It's a treasure trove of stories, poetry, and wisdom that continues to enrich the cultural tapestry of Morocco and inspire writers and readers alike, both within the country and beyond its borders.

Religion in Morocco: Islam's Influence

In the heart of North Africa lies Morocco, a country deeply rooted in Islamic tradition and culture. Religion, particularly Islam, plays a central role in the daily lives of Moroccans and is a fundamental aspect of the nation's identity.

The Dominance of Islam:

Morocco is predominantly a Muslim country, with over 99% of its population adhering to Islam. Sunni Islam is the prevailing branch followed by Moroccans, and the Maliki school of jurisprudence is the dominant Islamic legal tradition. This religious adherence influences virtually every facet of Moroccan society, shaping its traditions, values, and way of life.

Historical Islamic Roots:

The history of Islam in Morocco dates back to the 7th century when Arab armies brought the religion to North Africa. Morocco played a significant role in early Islamic history, serving as a center of learning and scholarship. The spread of Islam in Morocco led to the establishment of dynasties such as the Idrisids, Almoravids, Almohads, and Marinids, each contributing to the development and preservation of Islamic culture.

Islamic Architecture and Art:

One of the most visible expressions of Islam's influence in Morocco is its architecture and art. The country boasts a wealth of Islamic architectural masterpieces, from the intricate geometric patterns adorning mosques and madrasas to the stunning mosaics and calligraphy found in historic sites like the Medersa Ben Youssef in Marrakech and the Hassan II Mosque in Casablanca. The blending of Islamic, Andalusian, and Berber architectural styles has produced unique and breathtaking structures that stand as testaments to the country's rich heritage.

Islamic Holidays and Traditions:

Morocco celebrates a host of Islamic holidays with fervor and devotion. Ramadan, the holy month of fasting, is observed by Muslims throughout the country. During this time, Moroccans fast from sunrise to sunset, breaking their fast with the evening meal known as iftar. The Eid al-Fitr and Eid al-Adha festivals are also widely celebrated, marked by communal prayers, feasts, and acts of charity.

Religious Tolerance:

Morocco's Islamic identity coexists with a tradition of religious tolerance. The country has a small Christian and Jewish minority, and their places of worship, synagogues, and churches are respected and protected. The Moroccan constitution guarantees freedom of religion, and the nation is known for its religious pluralism and interfaith harmony.

Sufism and Spirituality:

Morocco has a rich Sufi tradition, with numerous Sufi brotherhoods or "tariqas" spread across the country. Sufism emphasizes the inner, spiritual dimension of Islam and encourages practices like chanting, dancing, and meditation as paths to spiritual growth. Many Moroccans are drawn to Sufi orders for spiritual guidance and community.

Islamic Education and Institutions:

Morocco places great emphasis on religious education. The country has a network of religious schools known as "madrasas" where students learn not only the Quran but also Islamic law, theology, and history. The University of Al-Qarawiyyin in Fez, founded in 859, is considered one of the oldest centers of Islamic learning in the world.

Islam's influence in Morocco is profound and pervasive, shaping the country's culture, architecture, traditions, and values. It's a dynamic and multifaceted force that has evolved over centuries, blending Arab, Berber, Andalusian, and African influences. Religion in Morocco is not just a matter of faith; it's a way of life, a source of identity, and a reflection of the nation's enduring commitment to its Islamic heritage.

Moroccan Education and Institutions

Morocco, with its rich cultural heritage and diverse population, places a high value on education. The Moroccan education system has evolved over the years, reflecting a blend of traditional Islamic teachings, European influences, and a commitment to modernization.

Education in Morocco is a fundamental right guaranteed by the constitution. The country has made significant progress in expanding access to education, particularly in the last few decades, and has achieved near-universal enrollment in primary education. However, there are still challenges to overcome, including disparities in access and quality.

The Moroccan education system is divided into several levels. Primary education, which is compulsory and free, provides the foundational knowledge and skills to students. Secondary education is divided into two cycles: the lower secondary cycle (Collège) and the upper secondary cycle (Lycée). Successful completion of the upper secondary cycle allows students to take the Baccalaureate exam, a prerequisite for entering higher education.

One of the notable features of the Moroccan education system is its bilingual nature. While Arabic is the primary language of instruction, French is also widely used, especially in higher education and in scientific and technical fields. This bilingualism reflects Morocco's historical ties with France and its desire to participate in the global economy.

Morocco boasts a number of universities and higher education institutions. The University of Al-Qarawiyyin in Fez, founded in 859, is considered the oldest existing, continually operating degree-granting university in the world. It has a rich history of scholarship and is a testament to Morocco's long-standing commitment to education.

In recent years, the Moroccan government has undertaken significant educational reforms aimed at improving the quality of education and aligning it with the needs of the job market. These reforms include modernizing curricula, expanding vocational training programs, and investing in infrastructure and technology.

Despite these efforts, challenges remain. Morocco faces issues such as high dropout rates, inadequate infrastructure, and a need for more qualified teachers. Additionally, there is a gap between urban and rural education, with rural areas often having limited access to quality education.

Nonetheless, Morocco's commitment to education is evident in its ongoing efforts to address these challenges and improve the educational opportunities available to its citizens. Education is seen as a pathway to economic development, social mobility, and a brighter future for the country, making it a central focus of Moroccan society and government.

Healthcare and Wellness in Morocco

In the mosaic of Morocco's diverse landscape, the threads of healthcare and wellness are woven into the fabric of daily life. The country has made significant strides in providing healthcare services to its citizens, balancing traditional practices with modern medicine to address the health and well-being of its population.

Morocco's healthcare system is a blend of public and private sectors, providing a range of medical services to its citizens. The Ministry of Health oversees the public healthcare system, which is accessible to the majority of Moroccans. The government has made efforts to expand access to healthcare, particularly in rural areas, through the construction of health centers and clinics.

Morocco's healthcare infrastructure includes modern hospitals and medical facilities, often concentrated in urban areas like Casablanca, Rabat, and Marrakech. These hospitals offer a wide range of medical services, including specialized care, surgery, and emergency services.

Traditional medicine, known as "herboristerie" or herbal medicine, continues to play a significant role in Moroccan healthcare. Many Moroccans rely on traditional healers and herbal remedies for common ailments and preventive care. Traditional Moroccan hammams, or bathhouses, are also places where wellness practices and relaxation are deeply ingrained in the culture.

One notable aspect of healthcare in Morocco is its commitment to maternal and child health. The country has made progress in reducing maternal and child mortality rates through initiatives that focus on prenatal care, vaccination programs, and improving access to healthcare for women and children.

Pharmacies are widespread in Morocco and play a crucial role in healthcare. Pharmacists are often highly trained and can provide advice and dispense medications for common ailments without a prescription.

Morocco has a national health insurance system that covers a portion of healthcare costs for citizens and residents. The government also provides subsidies for essential medicines to ensure affordability.

Despite these advancements, challenges persist in the Moroccan healthcare system. There is a need for improved healthcare infrastructure in rural areas, as access to medical services can be limited in remote regions. The healthcare workforce also faces shortages, particularly in specialized fields. Additionally, while progress has been made in healthcare, disparities in access and quality still exist.

Wellness in Morocco extends beyond healthcare facilities and practices. The country's natural beauty, from the Atlas Mountains to the Sahara Desert and the Atlantic coastline, offers opportunities for outdoor activities and relaxation. Moroccan cuisine, with its emphasis on fresh ingredients and aromatic spices, contributes to a healthy and flavorful diet.

The culture of Morocco encourages a balanced approach to life, emphasizing family, community, and the importance of rest and relaxation. Traditional practices like yoga, meditation, and herbal remedies are intertwined with daily life, promoting a holistic approach to well-being.

In summary, healthcare and wellness in Morocco are deeply rooted in tradition and modernity, with the government making efforts to improve access to healthcare services and promote well-being among its citizens. The country's unique blend of traditional practices and modern healthcare facilities reflects its commitment to ensuring the health and vitality of its people.

Transportation in Morocco: Trains, Taxis, and More

In the labyrinthine streets of Morocco's bustling cities and the winding roads that snake through its diverse landscapes, a vibrant tapestry of transportation options weaves together the nation. Navigating Morocco is an experience in itself, with a mix of modern and traditional modes of transportation.

Trains: The Moroccan railway system, operated by ONCF (Office National des Chemins de Fer), is a reliable and efficient way to travel across the country. It connects major cities like Casablanca, Rabat, Marrakech, and Tangier. The trains offer varying levels of comfort, from standard to first-class, and are known for their punctuality. Morocco's high-speed train, the Al-Boraq, has further improved connectivity, reducing travel times between cities.

Buses: Buses are a popular and economical means of transportation, especially for routes not covered by trains. Several bus companies operate services throughout Morocco, connecting cities, towns, and remote regions. Supratours and CTM are among the reputable bus companies known for their comfort and safety.

Grand Taxis: For shorter trips within cities and towns, as well as intercity travel, grand taxis are a common choice. These shared taxis are often old Mercedes-Benz sedans or station wagons and can accommodate up to six passengers. While not luxurious, they offer a cost-effective way to get around.

Petit Taxis: In Moroccan cities, smaller red taxis, known as "petit taxis," provide convenient local transportation. They are metered, and fares are relatively affordable for short distances within city limits. It's essential to ensure the meter is running to avoid any misunderstandings.

Horse-Drawn Carriages: In some cities like Marrakech and Fes, traditional horse-drawn carriages, or "caleches," are a charming and leisurely way to explore the historic medinas and tourist areas.

Shared Ride Apps: Like in many parts of the world, ride-sharing apps like Uber and Careem are gaining popularity in Moroccan cities. They offer a convenient and familiar way to book rides, particularly for tourists.

Air Travel: For longer distances, Morocco has several international airports, including Mohammed V International Airport in Casablanca and Marrakech Menara Airport. Royal Air Maroc, the country's flagship carrier, offers domestic and international flights, making air travel a viable option for those with longer distances to cover.

Ferries: Given Morocco's coastal location, ferries are essential for connecting to Spain and other Mediterranean countries. Tangier is a major ferry port, with regular services to Spain, Gibraltar, and other ports in the region.

Camels: In the vast expanses of the Sahara Desert, camels remain a vital mode of transportation for nomadic communities and for tourists looking to experience the desert's timeless allure.

Motorcycles and Scooters: In urban areas, motorcycles and scooters are a common sight, zipping through traffic-clogged streets. They offer an agile way to navigate the bustling cities, but caution is advised due to the often chaotic traffic.

Car Rentals: For those who prefer independence and flexibility, car rentals are widely available in Morocco. However, driving in Moroccan cities can be challenging due to congested traffic and narrow streets. Long-distance travel on well-maintained highways is a more comfortable experience.

Navigating the mosaic of Morocco's transportation options can be an adventure in itself, with each mode offering its own unique experiences and challenges. From the timeless allure of camel rides in the desert to the high-speed trains connecting modern cities, transportation in Morocco is a reflection of the country's diverse and dynamic character.

Moroccan Etiquette and Customs

In the vibrant tapestry of Moroccan culture, a rich tapestry of etiquette and customs weaves together the social fabric of this North African nation. Understanding and respecting these traditions is not only a mark of courtesy but also a gateway to deeper cultural immersion.

Greetings: Greetings in Morocco are warm and often involve physical contact. A typical greeting involves a handshake, and it is common for people of the same gender to exchange kisses on the cheek, starting with the left and then the right. Greetings are accompanied by phrases like "Salam alaikum" (peace be upon you), to which the response is "Wa alaikum salam" (and peace be upon you).

Hospitality: Moroccan hospitality is legendary. It's customary to offer guests tea, often mint tea, upon arrival. Refusing such an offer can be seen as impolite. If invited to someone's home, it's a sign of respect to bring a small gift, such as pastries or fruit. When dining in a Moroccan home, wait for the host to begin the meal before you start eating.

Dress Code: Dress modestly, especially in rural and conservative areas. While urban centers like Marrakech and Casablanca are more liberal in terms of attire, it's respectful to cover your shoulders and knees, particularly when visiting religious sites. Women may also consider wearing a headscarf in more conservative areas.

Shoes: Before entering a home, mosque, or certain shops, it's customary to remove your shoes. It's a sign of respect and cleanliness.

Ramadan: If you visit Morocco during Ramadan, be aware that it is a month of fasting from sunrise to sunset for Muslims. Out of respect, it's best not to eat, drink, or smoke in public during fasting hours. Many restaurants and cafes will be closed during the day but come alive at night.

Public Behavior: Public displays of affection should be limited, especially in rural and conservative areas, to avoid causing offense. Loud behavior and overt displays of anger or frustration are generally frowned upon.

Haggling: Bargaining, or haggling, is a common practice in Moroccan markets (souks). Sellers often start with higher prices, and negotiation is expected. It's part of the shopping experience, so embrace it with a smile and a friendly demeanor.

Respect for Religion: Morocco is predominantly Muslim, and Islam plays a significant role in daily life. When visiting mosques, non-Muslims are usually not allowed inside, but some historical mosques may permit guided tours. Dress modestly when visiting religious sites, and respect prayer times by avoiding loud activities.

Tipping: Tipping, or "baksheesh," is customary in Morocco, especially in the service industry. It's polite to tip waitstaff, tour guides, and other service providers. Tipping is often done in cash.

Language: While many Moroccans speak French and some English, the primary language is Arabic. Learning a few basic Arabic phrases can go a long way in showing respect for the local culture.

Time: Moroccans often have a more relaxed approach to time, and schedules can be fluid. Be patient and flexible in your arrangements.

By embracing and respecting these customs and etiquettes, visitors to Morocco can forge deeper connections with the country and its people. It's a way to not only experience the stunning landscapes and rich history but also to engage with the heart and soul of this culturally diverse nation.

Safety Tips for Travelers in Morocco

Morocco is a captivating and diverse destination that beckons travelers with its vibrant culture, stunning landscapes, and rich history. While the country offers a wealth of experiences, it's essential to prioritize safety to ensure a memorable and trouble-free visit. Here are some important safety tips for travelers in Morocco:

1. Respect Local Customs and Etiquette: Familiarize yourself with Moroccan customs and traditions. Dress modestly, especially in conservative areas, and be mindful of public behavior, particularly during religious events.

2. Be Cautious with Street Food: Moroccan street food is delicious, but exercise caution when choosing where to eat. Opt for busy food stalls with a high turnover of customers to reduce the risk of foodborne illnesses.

3. Stay Hydrated: Morocco can be hot, especially in the summer months. Drink plenty of bottled water to stay hydrated, and avoid tap water.

4. Bargain Wisely: Haggling is common in Moroccan markets, but do it with respect and a friendly attitude. Know the approximate value of items and be prepared to walk away if the price doesn't meet your budget.

5. Secure Your Belongings: Petty theft can occur in crowded areas and tourist spots. Keep your belongings secure, and use a money belt or hidden pouch for important documents and cash.

6. Use Reliable Transportation: Stick to reputable transportation options like registered taxis, official tour operators, and well-known bus companies. Always confirm prices before taking a taxi to avoid surprises.

7. Avoid Unlicensed Guides: When exploring historical sites or markets, be cautious of unofficial guides who may try to offer their services. It's safer to use licensed guides provided by reputable tour companies.

8. Respect Privacy: Morocco values privacy, so avoid taking photos of people without their permission, especially in rural areas. Always ask before photographing locals.

9. Health Precautions: Check if any vaccinations or health precautions are recommended or required before traveling to Morocco. It's advisable to have travel insurance that covers medical emergencies.

10. Stay Informed: Keep yourself informed about the current political and security situation in Morocco through reputable sources. While Morocco is generally safe, it's essential to be aware of any potential risks.

11. Be Wary of Scams: Like in many tourist destinations, scams can happen. Be cautious of individuals who approach you with unsolicited offers or requests for money. Stick to established businesses and services.

12. Respect Nature: If you plan to explore Morocco's natural wonders, such as the Sahara Desert or the Atlas Mountains, consider hiring a local guide who knows the area well. Respect the environment by not leaving trash behind and following Leave No Trace principles.

13. Learn Basic Phrases: While many Moroccans speak French and some English, learning a few basic Arabic phrases can be helpful and appreciated by locals.

14. Emergency Numbers: Familiarize yourself with local emergency numbers, including those for police (19), fire (15), and medical assistance (150).

Morocco is a country that rewards curious travelers with unforgettable experiences. By staying informed, respecting local customs, and taking common-sense precautions, you can enjoy all that Morocco has to offer while ensuring your safety and well-being during your journey.

Sustainable Tourism in Morocco

In the heart of North Africa lies a country where the past seamlessly merges with the present, and where breathtaking landscapes beckon travelers from around the world. Morocco, with its diverse culture, rich history, and stunning natural beauty, has become an increasingly popular destination for tourists seeking unique experiences. However, as the tourism industry thrives, so does the need for sustainable practices to preserve the very essence that makes Morocco so enchanting.

Preserving Natural Beauty: Morocco boasts an array of natural wonders, from the rolling dunes of the Sahara Desert to the rugged peaks of the Atlas Mountains and the pristine beaches along its coastline. Sustainable tourism in Morocco begins with the protection of these precious landscapes. Conservation efforts and responsible travel practices are crucial to maintaining the country's environmental diversity.

Eco-Friendly Accommodations: In response to the demand for sustainable travel, eco-friendly accommodations have sprouted across Morocco. These establishments prioritize energy conservation, waste reduction, and responsible water usage. Many riads (traditional Moroccan guesthouses), hotels, and lodges have adopted sustainable initiatives, such as solar power and water-saving systems.

Supporting Local Communities: Sustainable tourism in Morocco goes hand in hand with supporting local communities. Engaging with the local culture, purchasing handicrafts directly from artisans, and choosing locally owned accommodations and restaurants all contribute to the economic well-being of the Moroccan people.

Cultural Preservation: The essence of Morocco lies in its unique blend of cultures and traditions. Sustainable tourism places a premium on respecting and preserving this rich heritage. Visitors are encouraged to participate in cultural experiences that are authentic and respectful of local customs, such as traditional music and dance performances, cooking classes, and visits to local markets.

Responsible Adventure Travel: For those seeking adventure in Morocco's rugged landscapes, responsible trekking and desert excursions are vital. Local guides who are knowledgeable about the environment and committed to its preservation can provide rewarding experiences while minimizing the impact on fragile ecosystems.

Reducing Plastic Waste: Morocco, like many countries, faces challenges with plastic waste. Responsible travelers can contribute by reducing their plastic consumption, using reusable water bottles, and disposing of waste properly. Many eco-conscious businesses in Morocco are taking steps to reduce single-use plastics.

Respect for Wildlife: Morocco is home to unique wildlife, including the Barbary macaque in the Atlas Mountains and various bird species in its wetlands. Sustainable tourism encourages wildlife observation without disturbing or endangering these species. Visitors are reminded not to feed or approach wild animals and to respect protected areas.

Promoting Sustainable Transportation: Exploring Morocco often involves various modes of transportation. Sustainable travel practices include using public transportation, carpooling, and supporting initiatives that promote cleaner and more efficient transport options.

Community-Based Tourism: Community-based tourism initiatives empower local communities to share their culture and heritage with visitors while benefiting economically. These programs offer travelers the opportunity to engage with Moroccans on a personal level and contribute directly to local development.

Educational Initiatives: Sustainable tourism is also about raising awareness among travelers about the importance of responsible practices. Many tour operators and guides in Morocco incorporate educational components into their tours, fostering an appreciation for the environment and cultural preservation.

As travelers continue to be enchanted by Morocco's allure, the importance of sustainable tourism practices cannot be overstated. By embracing these principles, visitors can not only experience the beauty and culture of Morocco but also play a vital role in conserving the very essence of this remarkable country for generations to come.

Excursions and Day Trips: Beyond the Cities

As you explore the captivating cities of Morocco, it's worth venturing beyond the bustling medinas and vibrant souks to discover the hidden treasures that lie just a short journey away. Morocco offers a wealth of exciting excursions and day trips that will allow you to delve deeper into its diverse landscapes, culture, and history. Here, we'll unveil some of the most enticing excursions that beckon travelers to venture beyond the city limits.

1. Atlas Mountains: A day trip to the Atlas Mountains promises awe-inspiring vistas and the opportunity to immerse yourself in Berber culture. Visit the picturesque Ourika Valley, where you can hike to waterfalls, explore Berber villages, and savor a traditional meal with local families.

2. Sahara Desert: No visit to Morocco is complete without experiencing the Sahara Desert. Embark on a multi-day desert excursion from cities like Marrakech or Fes to witness the mesmerizing sand dunes, ride camels into the desert, and spend a night under the stars in a desert camp.

3. Essaouira: The coastal town of Essaouira, a UNESCO World Heritage site, is a perfect day trip from Marrakech. Explore its historic medina with its Portuguese and Berber influences, stroll along the scenic beach, and savor fresh seafood in the charming medina.

4. Aït Benhaddou: Aït Benhaddou is a stunning ancient kasbah (fortified village) that has served as a backdrop for numerous films and TV series. It's a UNESCO-listed site and makes for an intriguing day trip from Marrakech or Ouarzazate.

5. Ouzoud Waterfalls: Located in the Middle Atlas Mountains, the Ouzoud Waterfalls are Morocco's highest waterfalls. You can take a day trip from Marrakech to enjoy a hike to the falls, witness the resident Barbary macaques, and have lunch overlooking the cascading waters.

6. Chefchaouen: Known as the "Blue City" for its stunning blue-painted buildings, Chefchaouen is a day trip destination from cities like Fes or Tangier. Explore its charming streets, hike in the nearby Rif Mountains, and soak in the unique atmosphere.

7. Meknes and Volubilis: Discover the historical richness of Morocco by visiting Meknes, a UNESCO-listed imperial city, and nearby Volubilis, a well-preserved Roman archaeological site. Both destinations are easily accessible from Fes.

8. Agadir: If you're looking for a coastal escape, Agadir offers beautiful beaches, a modern marina, and a relaxed atmosphere. It's a convenient day trip from Marrakech or a great addition to your southern Morocco itinerary.

9. High Atlas Villages: Explore the charming Berber villages nestled in the High Atlas Mountains. A day trip or multi-day trek in this region offers a glimpse into traditional mountain life and stunning natural beauty.

10. Casablanca: While Casablanca is a major city in Morocco, it's often visited as a day trip from nearby cities like Rabat or Marrakech. Explore its modern architecture, vibrant nightlife, and the iconic Hassan II Mosque.

These excursions and day trips allow you to unravel the diverse tapestry of Morocco, revealing its rich cultural heritage, striking natural beauty, and intriguing history. Whether you're drawn to the tranquil coastal towns, the rugged mountain landscapes, or the serene desert vistas, Morocco's diverse offerings are sure to leave a lasting impression on your travel memories.

Adventure Tourism: Trekking and Desert Safaris

For travelers with an adventurous spirit, Morocco is a paradise waiting to be explored. Beyond its bustling cities and historic sites, this North African gem offers a world of outdoor adventures that will satisfy the thrill-seekers and nature enthusiasts alike. In this chapter, we delve into the heart-pounding experiences of trekking in the Atlas Mountains and embarking on desert safaris in the vast Sahara.

Trekking in the Atlas Mountains:

The Atlas Mountains, stretching across Morocco, provide a dramatic backdrop for those seeking to conquer challenging terrain and breathtaking heights. Whether you're an experienced mountaineer or a novice hiker, there's a trek for everyone in the Atlas.

- **Toubkal National Park:** Home to Mount Toubkal, North Africa's highest peak, this park offers a range of trekking options. Ascend to the summit for panoramic views or explore the surrounding valleys and Berber villages.
- **M'Goun Massif:** Known as the "Valley of Roses," the M'Goun Massif offers treks through stunning gorges, lush valleys, and terraced fields. The annual Rose Festival is a must-see event.
- **Tizi n'Test Pass:** Located near Marrakech, this pass offers shorter hikes and the chance to experience Berber culture in nearby villages.

- **Dades Valley and Todra Gorge:** Explore the unique landscapes of Dades Valley, known as the "Valley of a Thousand Kasbahs," and the impressive Todra Gorge with its towering rock walls.

Desert Safaris in the Sahara:

The Sahara Desert, one of the world's most iconic landscapes, beckons adventurers to traverse its vast expanse of sand dunes, oases, and remote villages. Desert safaris in Morocco offer a blend of excitement, cultural immersion, and natural beauty.

- **Camel Treks:** Riding a camel through the desert is an unforgettable experience. Camel treks can range from a few hours to several days, with nights spent in traditional desert camps under a blanket of stars.
- **Merzouga:** This desert village is a popular starting point for Sahara adventures. From here, you can explore the Erg Chebbi dunes and experience the magic of the desert.
- **Desert Camping:** Spend a night in a desert camp, where you'll enjoy traditional cuisine, music around the campfire, and the peaceful solitude of the Sahara.
- **Off-Road Adventures:** For those seeking more adrenaline, off-road 4x4 excursions across the desert offer a thrilling ride over the dunes.
- **Fossil Exploration:** The Sahara is rich in fossils, and enthusiasts can join guided tours to search for prehistoric treasures.
- **Remote Desert Villages:** Explore the remote villages that dot the desert landscape, meet nomadic communities, and gain insight into their way of life.

Adventure tourism in Morocco combines the thrill of exploration with the chance to immerse yourself in the country's natural wonders and cultural traditions. Whether you're conquering peaks in the Atlas Mountains or crossing the endless sands of the Sahara, these experiences will leave you with lasting memories and a profound appreciation for Morocco's diverse landscapes.

Morocco's Future: Challenges and Opportunities

As Morocco stands at the crossroads of the 21st century, it faces a myriad of challenges and opportunities that will shape its future trajectory. This North African nation, known for its rich history and diverse landscapes, is navigating a complex path toward modernity while preserving its cultural heritage. In this chapter, we examine the key factors, both internal and external, that will influence Morocco's future.

1. Economic Development:

Morocco's economy has been on a steady growth trajectory, driven by industries such as agriculture, tourism, manufacturing, and renewable energy. However, the nation faces the challenge of reducing income inequality, addressing youth unemployment, and diversifying its economic base.

2. Governance and Political Stability:

Morocco has made strides in political reforms, including a new constitution in 2011. However, ensuring political stability and strengthening democratic institutions remain ongoing challenges.

3. Education and Innovation:

Investments in education and research are essential for Morocco's future. The nation aims to foster innovation and develop a skilled workforce to compete in the global knowledge economy.

4. Energy Transition:

Morocco has been a pioneer in renewable energy, with projects like the Noor Solar Power Complex. The country's commitment to clean energy presents opportunities for sustainable development and reducing dependence on fossil fuels.

5. Environmental Conservation:

Preserving Morocco's natural beauty is critical. Initiatives for sustainable tourism, protection of biodiversity, and combating desertification are essential for the country's environmental future.

6. Infrastructure Development:

Investments in transportation, including high-speed railways and ports, are positioning Morocco as a regional hub for trade and connectivity.

7. Cultural Heritage Preservation:

As Morocco modernizes, it must also protect its rich cultural heritage. Balancing tradition and progress is a delicate task.

8. Regional Dynamics:

Morocco's relationships with neighboring countries and its role in regional organizations like the African Union will influence its future diplomacy and security.

9. Social Inclusion:

Ensuring the inclusion of marginalized groups, including rural communities and women, is crucial for social harmony and progress.

10. Geopolitical Considerations:

Morocco's strategic location at the crossroads of Europe and Africa makes it a key player in regional politics and security.

11. Tourism Growth:

Tourism is a vital sector, and Morocco's ability to attract visitors while maintaining cultural integrity will be pivotal.

12. Global Partnerships:

Morocco's international collaborations, including trade agreements and diplomatic alliances, will shape its global standing.

In conclusion, Morocco's future is a complex interplay of challenges and opportunities. As the nation strives to balance tradition and modernity, navigate economic and political transitions, and address social and environmental concerns, it does so with a rich tapestry of history and culture as its backdrop. The path forward for Morocco will be defined by its ability to adapt, innovate, and build a future that reflects the aspirations of its people while embracing its unique identity on the world stage.

Epilogue

As we come to the end of our journey through the rich and diverse tapestry of Morocco, it's worth reflecting on the extraordinary land we've explored together. Morocco, with its ancient history, captivating landscapes, vibrant culture, and warm hospitality, has left an indelible mark on our hearts and minds.

Throughout this book, we've delved into the intricate threads that make up the Moroccan story. We've traced the footsteps of early civilizations that once thrived on this North African soil, marveled at the architectural wonders of imperial cities, and sipped the fragrant tea that binds communities together. We've wandered through bustling souks, discovered the rhythm of Moroccan music and dance, and witnessed the fervor of religious celebrations.

In Morocco, the past seamlessly weaves into the present, where ancient traditions coexist with modern aspirations. The country's history, from the Berbers and Phoenicians to the Romans and Arabs, has created a rich mosaic of influences that define its identity today. Morocco's geographical diversity, from the rugged Atlas Mountains to the endless Sahara Desert and picturesque coastal towns, provides a stunning backdrop for this cultural tapestry.

We've savored the flavors of Moroccan cuisine, from tagines bursting with spices to the sweetness of pastries soaked in honey. We've marveled at the intricate artistry of henna tattoos, the elegance of traditional attire, and the warmth of Moroccan hospitality in riads and guesthouses.

Our journey has taken us to iconic cities like Marrakech, Fes, and Casablanca, each with its unique charm and history. We've explored hidden gems like Meknes and Chefchaouen, where history and beauty intersect in unexpected ways. We've wandered the serene streets of Essaouira and ventured into the mysteries of the Sahara Desert and the rugged Atlas Mountains.

Morocco's future is a story yet to be fully written, with challenges and opportunities that will shape its destiny. From economic growth and political stability to environmental conservation and cultural preservation, Morocco stands at a pivotal moment in its history.

As we bid farewell to Morocco, let us carry with us the enduring memories of this extraordinary land, the warm smiles of its people, the echoes of its music and the flavors of its cuisine. Morocco invites us to return, to continue exploring its depths, to immerse ourselves in its traditions, and to witness its ongoing evolution.

May the spirit of Morocco, a land of rich heritage and boundless possibilities, remain alive in our hearts, inspiring us to embrace the beauty of diversity, the power of tradition, and the promise of the future.

Printed in Poland
by Amazon Fulfillment
Poland Sp. z o.o., Wrocław